D0131415

CAUSES AND CONSEQUENCES

OF THE

GREAT DEPRESSION

CAUSES AND CONSEQUENCES

OF THE

GREAT
DEPRESSION

STEWART ROSS

RSVP

RAINTREE
STECK-VAUGHN
PUBLISHERS
The Steck-Vaughn Company

Austin, Texas

Published by Raintree Steck-Vaughn Publishers,
an imprint of Steck-Vaughn Company

Developed by the Creative Publishing Company
Editor: Helena Ramsay
Designed by Ian Winton

Raintree Steck-Vaughn Publishers staff
Project Manager: Joyce Spicer
Editors: Shirley Shalit, Pam Wells
Electronic Production: Scott Melcer

Consultant: Michael M. Morrogh, Shrewsbury School

DDS--99-3135

Cover photo (large): A New York City soup kitchen feeds the jobless in the early 1930's.
Cover photo (small): A photo of a typical prosperous couple at the height of the roaring twenties.

VR 2016

Library of Congress Cataloging-in-Publication Data

Ross, Stewart.
　Causes and consequences of the Great Depression / Stewart Ross.
　　　p.　　cm. — (Causes and consequences)
　Includes bibliographical references and index.
　Summary: Examines the reasons for the Great Depression, the events that happened during that period, and some of its tragic consequences.
　　ISBN 0-8172-4059-4
　　1. Depressions — 1929 — United States — Juvenile literature.
　[1. Depressions — 1929.]　I. Title.　II. Series.
　HB3717 1929.R65　　1998
　338.5'42–dc21　　　　　　　　　　　　　　　　　　97-26532
　　　　　　　　　　　　　　　　　　　　　　　　　　CIP　AC

Printed in Hong Kong
Bound in the United States
1 2 3 4 5 6 7 8 9 0 LB 01 00 99 98 97

CONTENTS

BLACK THURSDAY

TROUBLE AHEAD –
THE WALL STREET CRASH

During the 1920s most sectors of the U.S. economy enjoyed steady growth. As a result, from 1922 onward shares on the New York stock exchange rose in value. The climb continued for the next eight years, slowly at first but then more sharply. Many fortunes were made. Millions of small investors, with little money to spare, risked their savings hoping to cash in on the spectacular rise.

But no boom lasts forever. By 1929 cautious dealers warned that the good times were coming to a close. The Federal Reserve Board anxiously suggested that it was unwise for banks to lend money for speculation. Then, slowly at first, the market started to fall. At the start of the third week of October a cloud of uncertainty hung over Wall Street, the area of lower Manhattan in New York City where the American stock market is based.

On Monday, October 20, trading in shares was jittery. Nevertheless, some dealers went on buying. The price of shares had soared spectacularly during the spring and summer. While many expected the rise to continue, doom-peddlers urged caution. The fall, however, was closer than they had expected. And it was far more dramatic.

On Tuesday, October 21, share prices dipped. Nervousness grew. On Wednesday they fell again. Then, on Thursday, October 24 — "Black Thursday" — the crash began. By the end of the day, a record 12.9 million shares had been sold. (In 1926 the daily average had been between one and two million.) With so many shares for sale, prices plummeted. Those who bought believed they had a bargain. They soon realized their mistake.

"Black Thursday" marked the beginning of the greatest economic crisis ever to hit the modern world.

A dramatic depiction of "Black Thursday," October 24, 1929, the day prices collapsed on the New York stock market. Thousands of investors were ruined, and the world economy began to slide into the worst ever depression of modern times.

CRASH TO SLUMP

The Wall Street Crash continued until the end of October 1929. Share prices fell again on Monday, October 28. The next day, despite efforts by the federal government and the major banks to restore confidence, the downward spiral continued. Some 16 million shares changed hands, almost all for rock-bottom prices. Investors' losses were estimated at $26 billion.

The day-by-day falls were greater than anything previously experienced in U.S. history. A few desperate bankrupt brokers committed suicide. Some jumped from Manhattan's skyscrapers. Businessmen who had flaunted luxurious limousines and palatial houses at the start of year were now destitute. Ordinary middle-class families were forced to sell their homes — if they could find buyers — and take to the streets.

The shock waves of the collapse spread rapidly from New York to virtually all sectors of the U.S. economy. In every state, shops, farms, manufacturers and other enterprises — both large and small — went

My son and I have for some days been buying stocks and shares.

The U.S. multi-millionaire John Davison Rockefeller tries to restore confidence in the stock market, late October 1929.

A soup kitchen in Chicago. Men unemployed, lean and miserable, are given free food to prevent them from starving. By 1932 U.S. unemployment had risen to over 12 million.

bankrupt by the hundreds. Workers were laid off, swelling the pool of unemployed to a vast, hungry lake. The welfare services were swamped. The buoyant world of the 1920s, America's boom years, ended in the poverty, misery, and despair of the Depression.

U.S. politicians and economists had never experienced anything like it before. They were out of their depth, and the policies that they adopted were inadequate. Some actually made the situation worse. The U.S. economy was the most powerful in the world. Inevitably, therefore, events in America affected other nations around the globe.

American banks and financiers ceased to invest money overseas. Every dollar they had was needed to make good their losses at home. Firms that had previously exported to the U.S. suddenly found that there was no market for their goods. Stock markets all over the world followed Wall Street's downward slide. Prices of raw materials fell, bringing dire poverty to millions in nonindustrial countries. By Christmas, 1930, the American Depression had turned into a worldwide slump of horrifying proportions.

Industrial nations had always faced periodic economic downturns. Previously, however, they had been part of a cycle in which good and bad times followed each other. By 1932 it seemed as if the cycle had been broken and that the economy would not correct itself. But to the millions caught in a net of poverty not of their own making, the future looked just as bleak as the present. This atmosphere of despair had serious political consequences.

In the more stable democracies, such as the U.S. and Britain, administrations floundered but the political system survived. In countries where democracy was less deeply rooted, notably Germany and Japan, the Depression had a more sinister effect. Democracy itself was discredited, bringing to power regimes that were to plunge the world into devastating war.

When we consider . . . the losses from which the world suffers during a period of economic stagnation . . . , it is impossible not to be impressed by the almost absolute failure of society . . . to devise any means by which such disasters may be averted.

League of Nations report, 1930.

CAUSES AND CONSEQUENCES

The first half of this book looks at the causes of the Great Depression. The U.S. stock market collapsed because of over-production: American industry was turning out more goods than people could afford. But this raises more questions than it answers. What, for example, caused the over-production? Why did the Wall Street Crash trigger a major downturn in the U.S. economy? Why were banks and politicians unable to halt the slide into recession? Why did the slump last for so long and why did it spread around the globe?

The root of the problem lay in the economic system that emerged after World War I (1914-1918). Even today, historians and economists disagree over the details of the system's weaknesses. The basic flaws, however, are clearly understood.

The second half of the book is concerned with the nature and consequences of the Great Depression all over the world. It explores themes universal to all industrialized countries. These include the direct effects of the Depression, such as poverty and despair, the decline in world trade and effect of the slump on culture. The reaction of countries that were, or became, totalitarian and the full effect of the Depression on nonindustrialized nations and smaller democracies is also described.

Finally, the last chapter looks at the long-term consequences of the Depression. These continued to be felt long after World War II. Indeed, in modern governments' economic and welfare policies, they remain with us to this day.

THE IMPACT OF WAR

In order to understand the economic collapse of the early 1930s, we have to go back to the period before World War I. As soon as the war was over, Americans in every walk of life looked for a return to what they called "normalcy." By this they meant the conditions prevailing before the war. Following the shock of total war, the prewar years came to be seen as a sort of golden era when all had been right with the world. The government had kept to itself, and the average American had been free to pursue his or her own goals

America was not alone in regretting the passing of the prewar years. A French cartoon of August 1919 illustrates the cost of World War I (1914-1918) to the French nation. Weighed down by debt, the French certainly longed for a return to the "golden era" before the war.

in peace. Europe developed a similarly nostalgic view of the early part of the century.

Whether the first years of the twentieth century were golden or not, they were certainly happier and calmer than those that followed. The war shattered lives, dynasties, governments, industries, patterns of trade, and investment. The most significant result of this upheaval, as far as this book is concerned, was the creation of a far less stable economic system. It was this system that collapsed in 1929.

BEFORE THE WAR

Four aspects of the prewar world economy need emphasis. The first was growth. From the late 1880s to 1914 trade, manufacture, population, and agriculture all grew. In many ways they were related. A rising population, for example, led to a demand for more food, houses, and goods.

The countries that came late to industrialization expanded most quickly, because they were growing from a lower starting point. The best example is Russia, which made tremendous strides during the quarter century before World War I. The countries that had been first to industrialize, notably Britain, advanced the slowest. They were held back by outdated practices and machinery. The average rate of growth in Europe was about 1.5 percent per year. In the U.S. it was higher — averaging about 1.8 percent per year.

This brings us to the second point, the emergence of the U.S. as the world's wealthiest country. America had everything needed for rapid expansion — a large population, good transportation systems, fine education, political stability, abundant raw materials, and a government that had little wish to interfere in economic affairs. By 1913 the U.S. Gross National Product per person (or GNP, meaning the value of all the manufactured goods and services that a country produces) was five times the European average. It was 25 percent higher than Britain, the previous world leader. From this time onward, whatever happened in America was bound to affect the rest of the world.

Thirdly, by 1914 it is realistic to speak of a world economy. This was made possible by the invention of the telegraph and radio, the building of large, fast, and reliable steamships, and the spread of railroad systems through every continent. As a result, the great

An American primary school class in 1900. The last 30 years of the nineteenth century witnessed remarkable developments in public education in the U.S. Outside the South, most states made attendance compulsory and the national illiteracy rate fell from 17 percent to 11 percent.

industrial and agricultural nations produced for a world market. The first multinational companies, for example Ford Motors, appeared. By 1913, 50 percent of exports from the U.S., the most self-sufficient industrial giant, were manufactured goods.

Finally, world trade and manufacture were carried on in an atmosphere of great stability. Much of this was due to the influence of the stock market in London and Wall Street, two of the world's most important financial centers. The British currency, the pound sterling (£s), was virtually an international currency, like the U.S. dollar ($US) today. To ensure stability, dollars, like sterling and the German mark, were on the gold standard. This fixed the rate of exchange between paper money and gold. For every dollar in circulation, there was actual gold in the U.S. Department of the Treasury. In such a situation everyone knew precisely where the gold was held that backed the paper currency.

The United States and Britain were responsible for about 30 percent of global exports. The U.S. had tariffs on and off at various points, while Great Britain followed a policy of free trade. It had no tariffs on materials leaving or entering the country. Britain and some other industrial nations' free trade policy helped to make one huge market.

THE DISRUPTION OF WAR

After four years of war the old economic system was shattered forever. No matter how much people may have wanted it, a return to "normalcy" was impossible. Trade had been heavily disrupted and large areas of Europe had been devastated. Wartime governments had interfered as never before in economic affairs. Following a Communist revolution in the autumn of 1917, Russia had left the community of nations. The combatant states, with the exception of Japan and the U.S., were left with huge burdens of debt. By 1918 the U.S. was unchallenged master of the world economy.

Economic warfare was an essential aspect of World War I. The blockade was a key tactic. As soon as the war began, Britain and France set up a blockade of German ports using mines and surface ships. The Germans replied by using submarines to attack shipping trade with the Allies. These two moves destroyed prewar trade patterns at once. Hundreds of ships were sunk. Suppliers lost valuable cargoes. Bankers saw their investments sink to the bottom of the ocean. Factories ran short of vital raw materials.

The destruction on land was equally devastating. Although raids by airships and the early bombers did comparatively little damage, huge swaths of Belgium, Poland, northeastern France, and western Russia

The legacy of war — the shattered remains of La Bassée, one of hundreds of French villages destroyed during the war.

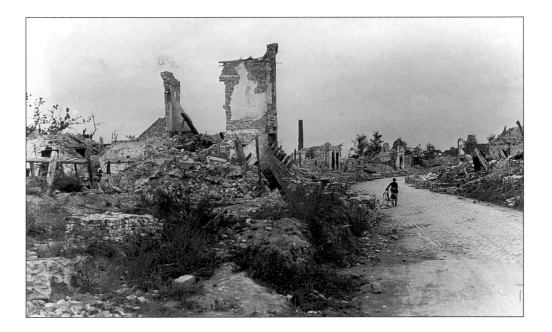

In order to limit consumption after World War I, all British citizens were issued ration books like these. The books contained coupons that had to be handed in when buying food or clothes.

A person shall not give employment to a workman who has within the previous six weeks . . . been employed on . . . munitions work.

A clause from the British Munitions Act (1916) that tried to prevent employees from leaving vital munitions work.

were flattened by constant artillery bombardment. As late as the 1970s, one ton of unexploded shells was still being lifted from Belgian soil every day. Owing to the German occupation of major French industrial areas, total steel production fell during the first years of the war.

To meet the needs of war, governments in all countries took unprecedented control over their economies. As a result, industrial manufacture on both sides was distorted. Production of consumer goods fell as workers were moved to munitions factories. The workforce of occupied Belgium was seriously depleted when 60 thousand people were deported to work in Germany. Businesses unable to switch to wartime needs saw prewar profits dwindle. Tariffs replaced free trade. Governments used rationing to limit the consumption of essential goods and foodstuffs. Inflation put a further brake on expenditure. Wartime prices doubled in Britain and France, and rose even more steeply in Germany.

Russia's Communist revolution and subsequent withdrawal from the war in 1918 had a worldwide impact. Foreign loans had underpinned Russia's prewar expansion. These loans, which came largely from France, were now lost forever. By 1918, the German seizures and the disruption caused by both international and civil war had taken their toll. Russian industrial output had been reduced to a mere 13 percent of its level in 1913.

The losses and destruction were uneven. European manufacturing output fell by 25 percent during the war, but worldwide it rose. Shipyards worked day and night to replace the vessels lost in the hostilities. In regions beyond the range of the guns, steel mills, iron and coal mines, textile factories, munitions works, and countless smaller workshops strained to meet the demands of the politicians and generals. During the war British steel production rose by some 30 percent, shipbuilding by 25 percent. In the fight for survival, no one considered how the wartime boom could be adapted to meet the needs of peace.

The business of the United States is business . . . The man who builds a factory builds a temple.

U.S. President Calvin Coolidge, 1925.

U.S. DOMINATION

Europe's economic turmoil was not matched in Japan or the U.S. Japan, which fought on the Allied side but suffered only minor losses, moved eagerly into markets abandoned by the West. So did the U.S., which did not enter the war until April 1917. Wall Street benefited from the closure of the London stock market during the first few months of war. The dollar rose when Britain abandoned the gold standard in 1914. American bankers made handsome profits from the loans they made to the Allies, especially Britain. Americans may have stayed out of the conflict for moral reasons, but neutrality had its financial benefits, too.

At the end of World War I Europe was exhausted. Millions of servicemen needed new employment. Industrial plants, adapted to supply the needs of war, had to be changed back to meet the needs of peacetime. Britain, the world banker in 1914, was heavily in debt. No longer backed by gold, its currency had lost its international position to the dollar. The delicate network of world trade and finance, which had operated so successfully for the quarter century prior to 1914, was in a shambles. The future growth and stability of the global economy was now in American hands.

Richer and richer — the glossy Sears, Roebuck catalog of 1927, a symbol of prosperous postwar America. While the rest of the industrial world struggled to pick itself up after the war, the U.S. consumer-led economy boomed.

Sears, Roebuck and Co., Chicago
Spring and Summer 1927

THE NEW SYSTEM

Economics is an inexact science, especially on a global scale. Politicians and bankers of the postwar era recognized that their economic world was less stable than that of their predecessors, but they were unsure why. Moreover, there was no organization willing or powerful enough to take a lead in the search for stability. The new League of Nations (founded in 1919 to foster international peace and cooperation) did not have the U.S., Germany, or the USSR as members. The League's Financial Committee had nothing like the influence of the present-day World Bank or International Monetary Fund. (See page 68.) The United States was both unwilling and unable to take over Britain's role as unofficial supervisor of world trade.

THE DOORMAT

A famous cartoon drawn by David Low in 1932. It shows Japan trampling over the powerless League of Nations. Apart from imposing sanctions, the League had no way of tackling militaristic aggression.

Among the most troublesome problems were the persistent threat of inflation, tariffs that hampered the free flow of goods, and fluctuations in the relative value of major currencies. The breakup of the Russian, Turkish, Austro-Hungarian, and German empires created political boundaries that made little economic sense. (See page 18.) Most important of all, the global economy failed to adapt wartime requirements to those of peace.

A British war veteran tries to beg a few cents on the streets of London. The sudden arrival of millions of ex-soldiers onto the labor market in 1919-1920 greatly increased the problem of unemployment.

OVERPRODUCTION AND UNCERTAINTY

As we saw in the previous chapter, war fed a massive increase in production, particularly outside Europe. With the fighting over, manufacturers struggled to find markets for their goods. During the war combatant nations, desperate for supplies, had been prepared to pay high prices for food and raw materials. Now that the fighting was over, prices fell back and remained depressed.

As a result, workers in mining and agriculture, especially those outside Europe and the U.S., could not afford to buy Western manufactured goods. Managers and company directors, eager to maintain profits, kept wages low. Lower wages meant lower spending. This, in turn, squeezed profits still further. Thus the cycle of recession was established.

The picture was not totally gloomy. In some areas the 1920s were years of prosperity. The U.S., for example, experienced rapid growth in most sectors of the economy apart from agriculture. Other countries enjoyed similar growth, but for shorter periods. Expansion, however, did not necessarily occur at the same time, and it was often short-lived. There was a general postwar boom, followed by downturn. The cycle was repeated in the second half of the decade. Although there had been recessions during the prewar period, the new pattern of short-term boom, then recession was unsettling.

Very few of us realize . . . the intensely unusual, unstable, complicated, unreliable, temporary nature of the economic organization by which Western Europe has lived for the last half century.

John Maynard Keynes, British economist, 1919.

NEW RESTRICTIONS

Some of the reasons for the new economic difficulties were political. The old empires had made little sense in racial or cultural terms, but they had been economic units. Between 1919 and 1920 they were broken up into several smaller states. The Austro-Hungarian Empire, for example, was broken up to create Austria, Hungary, Czechoslovakia and Yugoslavia. The frontiers of Germany were redrawn. Poland reappeared as an independent nation. This resulted in new frontier posts springing up all over the continent. Alongside them appeared customs offices, empowered to protect domestic production by imposing tariffs on imports. Steel mills were separated from the mines that had supplied them. The rich German coal deposits of the Saar, for example, were administered by the League of Nations, but the French were allowed to mine there.

A French soldier guards a coal train on its way from the Ruhr to Metz. When the Germans were unable to meet their reparation payments in 1922, French troops moved in and requisitioned valuable German minerals.

Ports no longer served their traditional industrial centers – the Baltic town of Danzig, for example, was given to Poland. German East Prussia was separated from the rest of Germany by a corridor of Polish territory. The breakup of the Austro-Hungarian Empire meant that the great railroad junctions of Prague, Vienna, and Budapest now served a primarily national network rather than a transcontinental one. Freight cars sent abroad invariably failed to return. At each international frontier, cargo was unloaded from one set of cars and placed on another.

The world's leading bankers, notably Norman Montagu of the Bank of England and Benjamin Strong of the Federal Reserve Bank of New York, believed that financiers, not politicians, could sort out the problems. However, "bankers' diplomacy" usually got no further than the conference stage. Individual nations were too tied up with solving their own problems to consider a worldwide strategy. Short-term projects took priority over the long-term ones.

Britain was no longer strong enough to take a lead on its own. Its debt to the U.S. totaled a bewildering $3.7 billion. The other ex-Allies were equally indebted. In 1922 their total debt to the U.S. stood at $11.5 billion. Although America had the resources to take over Britain's prewar role and tackle the problem, the prevailing mood was inward-looking. Had U.S. investment been pumped into the ailing world economy, lesser nations might have stabilized and world trade been put on a surer footing. Instead, a large part of U.S. capital was reinvested at home or in Central and South America. Happily, the mistake was not repeated after World War II, when the Marshall Plan enabled U.S. money to pour into war-torn Europe.

It is logical that the United States should do whatever it is able to do to assist in the return of normal economic health in the world, without which there can be no political stability and no assured peace.

U.S. Secretary of State George C. Marshall, speaking at Harvard University in June 1947, seeks to avoid the mistakes made at the end of World War I.

INFLATION

Another legacy of the war was inflation. In order to purchase the necessary military supplies, governments printed more money. Obviously, this made each bank note worth less and caused prices to rise. The value of the Italian lira fell from a ratio of 5 to $1 U.S. in 1914, to 28 to $1 U.S. in 1921. The value of the French franc fell by half this amount. The dollar held its value.

Nothing eats away at economic security more harmfully than inflation. Savings are worth less. Serious long-term planning is impossible. Investors go

Cheaper than wood. A German housewife about to light her stove with banknotes made worthless by hyperinflation.

for short-term gain, not steady income. All these problems afflicted the European economies in the postwar period. Economic instability spilled over into politics. People lost confidence in their governments and looked to extremist leaders for solutions. It was in this climate that Fascist Benito Mussolini was appointed Prime Minister of Italy in 1922.

Germany's economic problems were worst of all. Shortages, an excess of imports over exports and of government expenditure over income fueled unprecedented inflation. By 1923, 2,000 printing presses, operating 24 hours a day, were needed to keep up the supply of almost worthless banknotes. Shops closed at midday to raise prices. Shoppers swapped purses for wheelbarrows to carry their cash. At the height of the crisis $1U.S. was worth 4.2 trillion marks.

REPARATIONS AND TARIFFS

Behind Germany's problems lay reparation payments. The Treaty of Versailles (1919) declared that the war had been Germany's fault and that Germany should pay for the damage it had caused. Other defeated countries were made to pay, but the amount demanded of Germany was by far the highest. In 1921 it was fixed at $33.25 billion, plus interest. It was, of course, far more than Germany could afford.

The following year the country was racked by inflation and defaulted on its payments. French and Belgian troops occupied the German industrial district of the Ruhr. This only made Germany's problems worse. In 1930 German production of iron and steel was almost 33 percent lower than in 1910. At the outbreak of war Germany had been the most powerful industrial nation on the European continent. Its commerce played a vital part in world trade. Germany's postwar troubles could only hamper a general recovery.

To protect domestic producers, many countries abandoned free trade. When one government placed duties on imported goods, others retaliated by doing the same. This development assumed serious proportions in 1922, when the U.S. imposed the Fordney-McCumber Tariff to keep out cheap foreign imports. U.S. producers were artificially protected from competition, and the example was copied by others. It was hardly the way to return to the longed-for "normalcy".

Berliners scavenging for scraps in a city rubbish heap, 1919. Although the war was over, Germans continued to die at a horrifying rate from disease and malnutrition.

TROUBLED ECONOMIES

The Great Depression had its roots in the U.S. It spread rapidly worldwide because of American economic dominance and because the economies of the Old World never really recovered from the trauma of total war. They were, quite simply, not strong enough to withstand the shock waves blowing across the Atlantic. Once the Western economies were tumbling into recession, the rest of the world was bound to follow.

A perceptive cartoon of 1931, suggesting that European prosperity depended on a German recovery.

(Th. Th. Heine)

Solange das Herz krank ist, kann der Körper nicht genesen.
There's no recovery for the body as long as the heart is ailing.
Tant que le cœur est malade, pas de guérison possible.
Mientras el corazón continúe enfermo, no se puede restablecer la salud.

This chapter looks at the major economies outside the U.S. and explains why they were still so vulnerable in 1929. In the light of what we have learned so far, it is not difficult to understand why Germany and the other defeated nations remained weak. However, the failure of France and, more surprisingly, Britain to recover their prewar positions is less clear.

THE LOST LEADER — BRITAIN IN DECLINE

The industrial revolution began in Britain. For most of the 19th century British economic power made it the most powerful nation on Earth. The British Empire covered one-quarter of the land surface of the globe. British sterling was accepted universally. As late as 1914, Britain was still the world's leading financial, trading, and maritime power.

The British pound sterling — for so long the world's major trading currency — dies of a broken heart in 1931 when it is no longer backed by gold.

Britain's relative decline was not immediately obvious once the war was over. It had, after all, been one of the victorious nations. A sudden demand for goods that had not been available for four years set off a short postwar boom. British prices were lower than American, and transatlantic exports grew. In 1919 the exchange rate between the dollar and sterling, fixed during the war, was allowed to float, to find its own level. The value of the pound fell by some 25 percent, making British exports even more attractive.

It was too good to last. Overproduction of food and raw materials overseas led to a fall in their prices. Buyers had less money for British exports, which decreased. By the end of 1920, Britain was in a severe recession. Unemployment rose and remained over one million for the rest of the decade.

Although the country recovered, there was no return to the levels of prewar growth. Coal and iron output

A highly-qualified British war veteran dramatically draws attention to his unemployed status, in 1930. As traditional industries struggled to get contracts, British unemployment remained high throughout the interwar period.

Any person of 65 and upwards living alone with no resources except pension would in the year 1929 fall below the poverty line.

A report on poverty in London, 1930.

remained virtually static. Steel production fell between 1920 and 1930. So did the output and export of cotton goods. By 1925 the tonnage of shipping completed was 33 percent of that in 1920. It had not risen much by 1930. Newer industries, such as car manufacturers, did better. But they could not make up the shortfall.

As a major trading nation, Britain stuck to the policy of free trade. (For example, Britain did not follow the policies of the U.S. which imposed protective tariffs on goods.) This put it at the mercy of nations that were already imposing a high tariff rate. In 1925 Chancellor Winston Churchill also returned the pound to the gold standard. This may have stabilized the economy. But it created problems, too, in that it made British exports more expensive, encouraged cheaper imports, and added to unemployment. When the worldwide recession struck at the end of the decade, the British economy was even more vulnerable.

FRANCE AND GERMANY

France had industrialized later than Britain, and in 1914 it was still a very rural country. During the 1920s the country experienced rapid urbanization when agricultural workers moved into the towns. Technological advances, particularly the generation of hydroelectricity, assisted industrial development. So too did inflation. By

1926 the franc stood at 20 percent of its 1913 value, making French exports an attractive buy.

France's recovery was also assisted by the fact that much of its industrial plant was new, especially in areas devastated by the war. The most notable success was France's motor industry, led by the three giants, Renault, Citroën, and Peugeot. The Renault plant at Billancourt was the largest in Europe, and there were further assembly plants in Britain and Germany.

Until the mid-1920s German recovery was severely handicapped by political instability, hyperinflation, the burden of debt and reparation payments, and the Franco-Belgian occupation of the industrial region of the Ruhr. From 1925 onward, however, things began to settle down. The U.S. banker Charles G. Dawes came up with a plan to restructure the State Bank and lighten the burden of reparations (1924). Five years later reparations were further diminished along the lines suggested by another American, Owen D. Young.

As a result, the output of electricity and automobiles doubled in Germany. Coal production also rose,

An acquaintance of mine . . . came to Berlin from a suburb with his monthly salary to buy a pair of shoes for his baby; he could buy only a cup of coffee.

A German citizen recalls the effects of inflation.

PUNCH, OR THE LONDON CHARIVARI.—August 15, 1923.

THE EXCHANGE ASYLUM.

ROUBLE. "WHAT'S YOUR NAME?"
MARK. "MARK."
ROUBLE. "WHAT ARE YOU DOING?"
MARK. "FALLING."
ROUBLE. "WHAT'S YOUR FACE VALUE?"
MARK. "A SHILLING."
ROUBLE. "WHAT ARE YOU WORTH NOW?"
MARK. "TWENTY MILLION TO THE POUND."
ROUBLE. "COME INSIDE."
FRANC (*nervously*). "I'M NOT FEELING TOO SANE MYSELF."

What is money worth? A cartoon of 1923 in which the worthless and crazy Russian ruble befriends the almost equally worthless German mark. The French franc is not too sure of its value, either. Uncertain exchange rates between the major currencies greatly hampered international trade.

although the output of the older iron and steel industries never reached their prewar levels. Nevertheless, the cost of rebuilding shattered industries and stabilizing the currency was high. As late as 1929, unemployment still stood at 12 percent of the work force.

JAPAN AND THE REST OF THE WORLD

Throughout the war Japan exported more than it imported. This trend was reversed as soon as the fighting stopped, and cheap European exports became available once more. Despite a short postwar slump, the Japanese economy continued to grow steadily during the 1920s. By 1930 the country's GNP was 50 percent higher than it had been in 1920.

Like most other major economies, Japan suffered from inflation. The falling value of the yen helped exports but discouraged long-term investment. Even so, electricity generation and steel production grew at a healthy rate. To increase stability, in 1930 the value of the yen was held at the value of gold. Like Britain, however, Japan was a trading nation. Its prosperity depended on the health of the world economy. When the worldwide recession began to bite the following year, Japan proved as vulnerable to its effects as the older Western economies.

Under Communist rule Russia was largely immune from the economic troubles and tribulations of the rest of the world. Her withdrawal from the world market had three principal consequences. One was the loss of Ukrainian grain exports. The second was the writing off of the huge loans made to the prerevolutionary czarist government. The third was the removal of about 120 million potential consumers from the world market.

During World War I agricultural output in all combatant countries fell. In Germany, for example, it declined by 40 percent. The figure for Hungary was a staggering 75 percent. This, coupled with the wartime demand for every kind of raw material, from wood to copper, increased prosperity in the largely nonindustrialized parts of the world that supplied the West's basic needs. Once the war was over, however, home food production picked up. The demand for raw materials also declined. It was a vicious cycle. As the producers of non-manufactured goods, such as wood, cotton, tin, grew poorer, they were able to buy fewer manufactured products. It was a situation ripe for disaster.

We are fifty or a hundred years behind the advanced countries. We must make good this distance in ten years. Either we do it, or they will crush us.

The Soviet leader Joseph Stalin, 1931.

THE NEW ERA

In the 1920s America was the most exciting place on Earth. It was creative, dangerous, proud and, above all, rich. It was as if the war had proved something that Americans had suspected for some time — they were the most powerful and important people in the world. Their factories and movies, skyscrapers, music, and lifestyle set trends that others followed. And after a short postwar downturn, the nation's wealth went on growing year after year.

The image of the Roaring Twenties was largely false — the decade ended in catastrophe. But at the time the image was more powerful than reality. It hid the problems of agricultural depression, stagnation in the old industries, overproduction, personal debt, and the widening gap between rich and poor. There were prophets of doom, but their warnings were drowned out by the wail of the saxophone and the ring of the cash register. Until, of course, it was too late.

The optimism of 1920s America is shown in this romantic painting by Gerrit A. Beneker, entitled "The Builder." By 1930 the image had been shattered as U.S. unemployment soared and most building work ground to a halt.

THE NEW ECONOMY

In the chassis assembly line there are 45 separate operations . . . . On operation number 44 the radiator is filled with water and on operation number 45 the car drives on to the road.

Henry Ford describing the assembly line production of his famous Model T car.

The Age of the Automobile. Model T Fords lined up ready for delivery, 1925. Although the auto industry flourished as never before during the 1920s, its success masked the sluggish performance of older industries, such as agriculture and coal.

The U.S. economy not only produced the goods, but it did so in a new way. By the mid-1920s the production of goods and services was crisscrossed with a network of interest groups. Coal producers, shoe manufacturers, farmers, shopkeepers — business people of all types banded together for cooperation, stability, and profit. The largest industries, notably automobiles, the railroads, and steel, were dominated by a handful of gigantic corporations. These groups of companies were called oligopolies. Ford and General Motors were the uncrowned kings of the automobile industry, just as United States Steel led the steel industry.

New techniques of "scientific" management spread to even the most modest businesses. Each had its planning, purchasing, finance, management, and production departments. Rule of thumb was out, the rule of financial efficiency was in. Workers were no longer mere cogs in the production process. The new thinking stipulated that a happy work force would be more productive. Contented workers were also less interested in joining trade unions. As a result, strikes declined. Even the old antibusiness labor leaders were converted. American capitalism, said former Socialist Party leader John Spargo, provided "the greatest hope for mankind."

Herbert Hoover (1874-1964) on the campaign trail, 1928. A rugged individualist bitterly opposed to federal intervention in business and finance, he said in his inaugural address that America's future was "bright with hope." Few forecasts have proved so disastrously wrong.

The federal government, which during the war had taken unprecedented control over production and distribution, backed off. The Republican administrations of Warren Harding (1921-1923), Calvin Coolidge (1923-1929), and Herbert Hoover (1929-33) saw their task as assisting industry, not directing it. The famous American journalist Walter Lippmann went so far as to deride President Coolidge for having a "grim, determined, alert inactivity which keeps [him]... busy all the time."

President Hoover's Department of Commerce began standardizing the sizes of basic items (such as wood screws) and publishing business statistics. Other federal departments adopted similar programs. Instead of restricting corporate cooperation, the independent commissions, such as the Interstate Commerce Commission, were arranging corporate cooperation. In keeping with the mood of the times, the Supreme Court favored oligopolies, trade associations, and limited union power.

The great issue before the American people today is the control of government and industry by private monopoly.

The Progressive Party Platform for the 1924 election.

NEW WEALTH

The U.S. economy experienced a small recession between 1921 and 1922. Exports fell in this period, as cheap European goods came onto the market again. Thereafter, it was growth virtually all the way. Over the decade the GNP rose by an average 5 percent a year.

This postcard of the late 1930s shows the Empire State Building. For a long time the tallest skyscraper in the world, the building was a brave symbol of U.S. postwar prosperity. Ironically, it was completed in 1931, at the height of the Depression.

Automobile output tripled between 1915 and 1925. In 1920 there were 8 million cars on the roads in the U.S. By 1930 the figure had risen to 23 million. The building industry, symbolized by Manhattan's mighty Empire State Building, also boomed. During the 1920s total U.S. manufacturing output rose by an impressive 64 percent. The rest of the world could only stand and marvel.

Production methods were revolutionized by the moving assembly line, pioneered by Henry Ford. The use of oil and electric power greatly increased productivity. All this was underpinned by a huge national investment in education. The proportion of young people going on to further education in the U.S. far outstripped that of its competitors. Only Germany had relatively more students of science and technology.

WARNINGS

The crash of 1929 and the slump that followed came as a total surprise to most Americans. It need not have been so. During the summer of 1929 professional brokers were noticing ripples of uncertainty in the stock market. Their causes were not too hard to uncover — for those who cared to look closely.

The boom of the 1920s was not evenly distributed. The heavy industries that had launched U.S. prosperity in the previous century — coal, iron and steel, ship building, cotton and agriculture — had lagged behind the newer, consumer-based ones. Wages had increased from an average of $1,308 a year to $1,716, but the swelling national income was distributed ever less evenly. Taxes on incomes over $1 million were cut from $600,000 to $200,000 between 1924 and 1928. Struggling to find money to pay the rent and meet the cost of basic necessities, working-class Americans could not afford many of the consumer goods that glittered on the shelves. There was a limit to the number of automobiles, electric irons, and refrigerators that the moderately well-off could buy.

Many middle-class families, lured by smart advertising, were also heavily in debt. Consumer credit (to use the modern phrase) was out of control. Speculation on the stock market further reduced spending power. But the factories went on producing and the banks went on lending. Somehow, sometime it had to stop.

The federal government, wedded to the hands-off ideals of the new era, ignored the signs of impending doom. It was not their job, they argued, to become involved in the day-to-day running of the economy. Individual citizens, firms, and corporations could sort things out by themselves, just as they had done since the war.

If there was no help at home, there was even less abroad. As we have seen, prices of raw materials were depressingly low. The grain farmers of Canada, sheep ranchers of Australia, and miners of Africa and Asia had no money to spend on American products. Neither had most Europeans. So, when the U.S. consumer stopped buying, the factories stopped running.

CRASH TO DEPRESSION

Although most economies had managed to readjust after the dislocation and destruction of total war, prewar global economic stability had not returned. World trade did not flow as easily as it once had. Moreover, serious weaknesses marked the financial and industrial sectors of many countries. These factors made it likely that a worldwide recession would have devastating effects.

But was such a recession likely? On the surface, no. The world's largest economy, the U.S., performed well for most of the 1920s. Confidence was high, but as we know, much of it was misplaced.

THE PRICE OF SHARES

Lacking central direction, the American financial system was out of control. During 1928 and the first half of 1929, the stock market boomed. Share prices rose 38 percent in 1928 and continued to climb. Amid all this heady growth, many investors lost sight of what a share really is.

Essentially, by buying a share in a company, the purchaser becomes owner of a part of the company and lends it money in return for a share of its profits (a dividend). The greater the profits are expected to be, the higher the value of the share. In the later 1920s, however, millions of shares were bought, not for the dividend they might bring, but because the purchaser hoped they could be sold for more than was paid for them. (This gambling, or speculation, with share prices always goes on. In the later 1920s, however, it reached almost manic proportions.)

The higher a share rose in value, the more investors thought it was a good buy. This meant that they bought still more shares. The trouble was that share prices climbed way beyond their real value in terms of the dividends they might produce. By 1928, demand for manufactured goods was falling off. This was just

Club Life in America. A 1929 cartoon from Judge *magazine suggests the different ways in which once-wealthy stockbrokers plan to kill themselves now that they have lost everything in the Wall Street Crash.*

when share prices were escalating most rapidly. There was a recession on the horizon.

To make matters worse, because the stock market appeared to offer easy income gains, Americans were tending to buy shares, instead of making long-term investments at home or overseas. This lack of secure investment reduced the spending power of those who might have bought surplus goods. In other words, the rocketing stock market was making a crash all the more inevitable. This brings us back to "Black Thursday," the day when 12 million shares were sold on Wall Street.

We now have to analyze why events on Wall Street had such a devastating side effect, not only in the U.S. but all over the world.

Only the very poor had nothing to lose . . . . Automobile companies simply let half their workers go. There were skyscrapers just finished that had no tenants. There were truckers with nothing to truck.

Alistair Cooke, journalist and broadcaster, newly arrived in the U.S. from England, 1929.

THE SLIDE CONTINUES

The extent to which the U.S. had been gripped by stock market fever became apparent only when prices started to fall. Nine million Americans had invested in

Unemployed U.S. veterans marched to Washington in 1932. They planned to go to the White House and urge the president to pay the bonus promised to them for their service in World War I. Before they could achieve this aim, the 9,000 strong "Bonus Army" was dispersed by federal troops, and four marchers were killed.

stocks and shares. A huge amount of the nation's surplus money had been plowed into the stock exchange. Banks, too, had risked investors' money in shares. As share prices fell, the surplus money disappeared. There was no spare money available to launch new enterprises, modernize old ones, or tide shaky ones over difficult periods. Businesses, starved of investment, began to fold. Economic activity slowed down.

The activities of the banks made the problem worse. Many lost money in the crash. To make up their losses, they called back the loans they had made. Businesses, farms, and houses were sold to repay the banks. If no buyer could be found, or if the price did not cover the amount of the loan, the borrower went bankrupt. The banks, therefore, never got their money back. Between 1930 and 1933 almost 9,000 banks went bankrupt. Investors lost everything.

As banks, businesses, and farms closed, unemployment rose. By 1933 some 30 percent of the work force of the U.S. was without work. In some areas the figure climbed to 50 percent or higher. Obviously, the unemployed had no money to spend on anything

American farmers pour unwanted milk into the road, 1932. Because of falling prices, receipts from sales did not cover the cost of bottling and transporting.

other than bare necessities for living. Consequently, the demand for all products, from cars to clothes, fell. Factories either cut back production or shut down completely. Unemployment rose further, so therefore did closures and bankruptcies as well.

Between 1929 and 1933 the U.S. economy shrank by 50 percent. The Wall Street Crash had become the Great Depression.

Of New England's 280,000 textile mill hands, 120,000 had no work a year after the crash.

U.S. historian Henry Steele Commager looks back at the Great Depression, 1978.

COULD IT HAVE BEEN AVOIDED?

In the U.S., only the onset of World War II really ended the Great Depression. As in the previous war, demand soared. Production rose to meet it, men and women went back to work, spending increased, and a decade of misery came to an end.

Today the lesson is clear: the way out of a slump of falling prices and production is for the government to borrow money and to spend. This "primes the pump" of the economy and gets activity going again. But during the 1930s this was a new and daring suggestion.

Traditional wisdom said that if a government borrowed during a recession, it only made matters worse. Conventional economics demanded government cuts, not spending. In Germany, however, the Depression had ended much earlier because Hitler's Nazi government had launched massive public spending programs, including rearmament.

One way out. Nazi spending on the armed forces brought Germany out of the Great Depression more quickly than most other industrialized countries.

The economic world is very far from simple and any single explanation [of the Depression] seems to me to be almost certainly wrong by the very fact that it is single.

Brazilian architect Otto Niemeyer, 1930.

One of the few economists to challenge the traditional view, the Englishman J. M. Keynes, was not widely listened to until the publication of his book *The General Theory of Employment, Interest, and Money* in 1936.

Keynes saw that national economies needed national direction. Only the central government could provide this. Both President Hoover and, to a lesser extent, President Franklin D. Roosevelt, shied away from taking such a step. Hoover had never liked financiers, and he was not too upset when share prices began to fall. His attitude changed, however, as the recession deepened. He called meetings of corporations and trade associations and got them to accept common policies. He persuaded companies to avoid mass layoffs. More helpful, he allowed the Federal Farm Board (set up in 1916 to help poverty-stricken farmers) to increase loans to distressed farmers. In 1932 he set up a Reconstruction Finance Corporation. It lent $1.5 billion to private business and then ran out of funds.

Hoover worked hard but to little effect. The Reconstruction Finance Corporation represented a leap in political philosophy. However, the relief that it offered was directed toward corporations, not toward individuals as it would be in F. D. Roosevelt's New Deal.

The Depression continued to deepen. Cotton went unpicked. Corn was burned in the fields. The lines at soup kitchens set up to feed the unemployed grew longer and longer. The Hawley-Smoot Tariff replaced the Fordney-McCumber Tariff in 1930. Intended to protect the U.S. from foreign competition, the new tariff only succeeded in making matters worse. Import duties now stood at 50 percent, and this provoked foreign governments to respond with high import tariffs of their own. Something could have been done to halt the downward spiral, and there were those who knew what it was. But in the grim days of the Depression the country's leaders looked to the past for answers, not the future.

A U.S. worker and his family on the road looking for work, 1938. The plight of such men and women was most movingly portrayed in John Steinbeck's novel, The Grapes of Wrath (1939).

THE RECESSION SPREADS

The first sign that all was not well with the U.S. economy came in 1928, when American loans overseas began to be reduced. The effect was doubly hard, as a similar policy was being followed in both Britain and France. Germany, which relied on American loans to finance reparation payments, was hit hardest of all.

Then came the Wall Street Crash and America's swift slide into recession. Once again, U.S. overseas investment was cut or even recalled. Between 1924 and 1929 the U.S. had invested $6.4 billion abroad. Most of it was in short-term loans, that could be called back in time of crisis — 1929 was such a time. From the end of 1930 onward, U.S. overseas investment averaged only $60 million a year, compared with $200 million in 1929.

Furthermore, the shrinking of the large U.S. market affected many exporters of both raw materials and finished goods. Banks in Britain, France, and Switzerland started to follow the American example and demand repayment of the loans they had made. Businesses went bankrupt, factories closed, and unemployment rose.

Finally, the Hawley-Smoot Tariff made it even harder for countries that had exported to the U.S. to earn dollars with which to repay their loans. The recession deepened worldwide. In January 1931, Bolivia failed to meet its foreign debt repayments. Other countries soon followed suit. In May the largest bank in Austria collapsed. The following month the German government declared itself unable to make reparation payments. Britain, having rejoined the gold standard six years earlier, finally left it forever in 1931. The Great Depression was now a worldwide phenomenon.

"How much can the German donkey carry?" A 1927 cartoon suggesting that war reparations placed an unfair burden on Germany. German resentment at the country's treatment by the international community helps explain the popularity of the Nazis.

CAPITALISM IN CRISIS

The Great Depression spread like a plague over the planet. Only the USSR and peoples living in the most primitive circumstances were unaffected by it. Just as it had no sudden beginning, so it came to no quick or definite end. Some countries, such as Germany, were free from its clutches by the mid-1930s. Others went on suffering to the end of the decade and beyond.

The Great Depression had an impact on all aspects of life. Its effects were not just financial and commercial. The very fabric of civilized society was shaken. Politics, culture, and even philosophy were changed by it. It shattered individual lives, destroyed faith in the system that had brought it about, and fed extremism of every kind. Most alarming of all in the long term, it reopened the wounds of World War I, which had just begun to heal.

In this chapter we look at the most immediate and universal effects of the Depression — economic decline and the near collapse of the capitalist system.

FINANCIAL CHAOS

When the crisis first hit, governments strove to maintain the value of their currencies. They were afraid that if their currency fell, inflation and the price of imports would rise. Their efforts were in vain. Despite pleas from the leaders of other Western nations, the U.S. dollar finally came off the gold standard in March 1933. The international system of backing currency with gold was gone forever, and the U.S. was blamed for this contribution to the deepening recession.

During the later 1920s the dollar and pound, both tied to gold, had been universal currencies to which the value of other currencies were linked. This helped international trade. With the collapse of this convenient mechanism by the end of 1933, the world's currencies divided into five major blocs. Some were still linked to gold (France, Switzerland, Italy, and much of northern

Africa). Others were tied to the U.S. dollar (U.S., Canada, and several countries in Central and South America), the pound sterling (Britain, Argentina, and most of the countries of the British Empire), the yen (Japan and Korea), or the German mark (Germany, much of Eastern Europe, Brazil, and other parts of South America).

Without a common currency arrangement, trade suffered. It was further hampered by the "tariff war" (also known as "protectionism") that followed the U.S.'s Hawley-Smoot Tariff of 1930. Germany and France limited the amount of goods allowed to come into their countries. In 1931 Britain ended its long attachment to free trade by putting 50 percent duties on 23 types of imports. At the Ottawa British Empire Conference in Canada, members of the empire agreed to a policy of "Imperial Preference." This gave favorable terms to trade within the empire, but penalized outsiders.

All these measures made a swift revival of international trade virtually impossible.

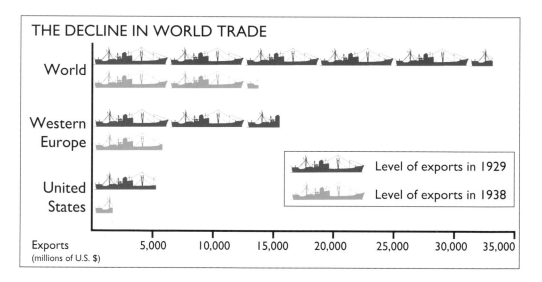

THE DECLINE IN WORLD TRADE

World

Western Europe

United States

Level of exports in 1929
Level of exports in 1938

Exports (millions of U.S. $)   5,000   10,000   15,000   20,000   25,000   30,000   35,000

Between 1929 and 1932 world trade fell by 66 percent. It had still not recovered to the preslump level by 1939.

INDUSTRIAL DECLINE

The raw statistics of the international Depression make alarming reading. Worldwide industrial production had fallen 40 percent by the end of 1933. In Britain and the U.S. the figure was over 50 percent. GNP in the 16 major economies fell 17 percent. In Poland it fell 25 percent. In 1933, GNP in the U.S. was at the 1913 level.

Many Third World countries, underdeveloped nations, that exported raw materials were badly hit. In several countries their earnings from exports were halved. The collapse did not affect all countries or commodities equally. Sri Lanka was struck by the fall in tea prices. The Brazilians burned coffee in their railroad engines to keep prices up. The prices of meat and dairy products, however, remained steady, sheltering New Zealand from the worst effects of the Depression. Oil, copper, and cocoa prices also held up well.

By and large, though, prices tumbled. The average cost of all farm products went down by 50 percent, bankrupting thousands of grain producers in the U.S. and Canada. Industrial prices fell by 33 percent. Traditional heavy industries were hardest hit. German steel production, for example, declined 66 percent. Newer manufacturers, such as those in the car industry, declined less and were the first to recover.

UNEMPLOYMENT

The most enduring image of the Great Depression is the unemployed worker, idle, dejected, uncomprehending. Unemployment was most noticeable in the cities of the West, where every day long lines formed at the employment offices and relief agencies. In the Third World, where most workers still lived in small village communities, the problem was not as obvious. Nonetheless, it was just as real.

At the height of the crisis, in 1933, 30 percent of employable Americans had no work. The situation was even worse in Germany, where there were 8 million unemployed by late 1932. This represented more than one-third of all workers. The situation was similar in both Denmark and Norway. Czechoslovakian unemployment rose from 39,000 in 1928 to 686,000 in 1935. Those who did have jobs were often given shorter hours and therefore earned less. In 1932 two-thirds of the German work force did

Industrial and human depression, Wigan, England, 1939. Children play innocently beside the dejected figure of an unemployed worker who is wearing wooden clogs for shoes. In the 1930s painful scenes like this were common throughout the industrialized world.

not work full-time. Women were sometimes employed in place of men, because they could be paid lower wages.

Figures cannot begin to tell the full story of unemployment. Loss of work meant a loss of self-esteem and a much lower standard of living, perhaps even starvation. Health declined and the birthrate fell. If workers who lost their jobs had families, they too were forced into poverty. The stores where they bought their goods took in less money. Governments and charities handed out relief that might, in happier times, have been invested in future prosperity. During the Great Depression charitable donations in the U.S. rose eightfold. Normally law-abiding citizens turned to petty crime to get money or basic necessities.

Unemployment was a terrible, obvious waste of skills, of money, of education, of energy, of ideas, of hopes and dreams — a waste of lives. Men and women grew understandably angry at the futility of it all. They blamed business, the government, racial minorities, bosses, bankers. In other words, they blamed the system that had allowed it to happen. Inevitably, the Great Depression had serious political consequences.

The last thing I saw on the night I left Seattle was numbers of women searching for scraps of food in the refuse piles . . . . While Oregon sheep raisers fed mutton to the buzzards I saw men picking for meat scraps in the garbage cans in the cities of New York and Chicago.

Oscar Ameringer, an editor, testified before a House Committee on Labor about his three-month tour that covered some 20 states.

A cartoon by Johnson in the German magazine Kladderadatsch, *1930. Still delighting in revenge, a French soldier roars with laughter at the efforts of Germany to get its industry going again. Before too long, Nazi aggression had turned the mirth to tears.*

GRAPES OF WRATH

The Great Depression was the most profound and
long-lasting recession of modern times. It is impossible to say precisely when it ended, because in 1939
the disruption it brought about merged with the chaos
of war. Nevertheless, by the mid-1950s the world economy was once again enjoying a period of sustained
growth. Commerce and manufacturing were growing,
and unemployment was lower than it had been in the
prewar years. There would be future recessions, such
as the one that occured in the late 1980s and early
1990s, but they would come nowhere near the scale of
the slump of the 1930s.

The direct effects of the Depression — financial
collapse, unemployment, and the shrinking of commerce — disappeared when the global economy picked
up. The indirect effects — social, political, cultural, and
intellectual — could not be so simply wiped away. The
Great Depression acted as a catalyst, forcing changes
in virtually all areas of human activity. In some areas,
the legacy is still with us. (See the final chapter.) This
chapter focuses on the Depression's more immediate
effects outside the area of economics.

THE NEW ECONOMIES

The Great Depression had a huge impact on the science of economics. Before the slump "economic liberalism" had guided most economic thinking. Three of its
central principles were:
(a) The basic capitalist laws of supply and demand made
the world economy self-regulating. (The greater the supply, the less the demand would be.) Recovery would auto-
matically follow recession, as night follows day.
(b) The task of government was simply to maintain a
"level playing field" on which capitalist business could
compete. If it entered the market by, say, subsidizing
the railroads, it caused more problems than it solved
because it broke the laws of supply and demand.

(c) The way to tackle unemployment was to cut wages so that more workers could be taken on.

The new theory, which owed much to the work of the British economist John Maynard Keynes, became known as the "managed" or "mixed" economy. This held, among other things, that:

(a) Unchecked capitalism, operating through the laws of supply and demand, did not guarantee growth. The Great Depression was the perfect example of this.

(b) Therefore governments needed to do more than just prepare the right conditions for business. In certain circumstances, such as occurred in the 1930s, it was their duty to intervene actively to guide the economic system.

(c) Unemployment was not necessarily reduced by cutting wages; this might reduce demand for goods and services further and lead to even higher unemployment. The way out of the cycle was to put money into the economy to increase demand for goods and services.

It took some time for Keynesian economics to catch on. There had been recessions before and things had recovered of their own accord. Not until 1931 did politicians accept that the Great Depression was something different. Secondly, with the extreme example of postwar Germany fresh in their minds, politicians were afraid of boosting their economies artificially in case they fueled inflation. Finally, a managed economy was associated with communism — it was, after all, the way economic affairs were run in the USSR.

In the end, however, things got so bad that government intervention seemed the only alternative to total collapse and even revolution. The way individual governments reacted to this situation is the subject of the next four chapters.

> The important thing for a government is not to do things which individuals are doing already . . . but to do those things which at present are not done at all.
>
> *British economist, John Maynard Keynes, 1926.*

THE NEW POLITICS

The horrors of World War I bred a new spirit of international cooperation. There were notable exceptions, such as the isolationism of the U.S. and the USSR. But many other world leaders expressed the hope that the postwar era would be one in which nations worked with rather than against each other in the search for peace and prosperity. This faith found practical expression in the League of Nations.

This mood of internationalism, already wearing thin by 1930, was one of the major casualties of the Great Depression. One of its last demonstrations was the World Economic Conference held in London in 1933 to find common policies to tackle the economic crisis. It broke up after three weeks with nothing agreed.

The League of Nations was too weak to provide leadership in economic matters. As early as 1919, the U.S. had declined membership, showing a tendency toward isolationism. Other powerful nations were too preoccupied with setting their own houses in order to find time to look for a global solution to their ills.

Troubled by unemployment and political unrest, it was each government for itself. As we have seen, tariffs in one country led to retaliatory tariffs in others. When one country lowered the value of its currency in relation to the currencies of other countries (devaluation), others were forced to do the same in order to remain competitive. In the chaos, it was easy to blame outsiders or foreigners for a country's woes. In Germany, the Nazis pointed the finger at Jews and at those who had drawn up the harsh terms of the Treaty of Versailles. The French blamed the Americans for negotiating easier reparation payments. In India, the British were blamed for paying less for their crops.

As a result, nationalism increased. Leaders such as Hitler, who were prepared to take advantage of this

Texan representative Martin Dies examines anti-Semitic propaganda brought into the U.S. by Nazi sympathizers. German attempts to blame the Jews for causing the Great Depression found a few prejudiced supporters even in the U.S.

WORLD'S HIGHEST STANDARD OF LIVING

There's no way like the American Way

Casualties of the free market. The poor stand in line for relief before a poster proudly announcing U.S. prosperity, 1937. At a national level, unemployment figures for African-Americans averaged about 50 percent higher than those for whites.

If all economists were laid end to end, they would not reach a conclusion.

Attributed to George Bernard Shaw, Irish dramatist and author, who was one of the intellectuals attracted to dictatorship in the 1930s.

kind of prejudice, swept to power. Thanks to the Great Depression, the world became a more dangerous place.

The Depression brought down almost every government that had been in power when it began. Coalition governments were formed in Britain and France; President Hoover lost the 1932 election; and the military increased their influence in political affairs in Japan. Throughout the democratic world, extremist groups of both the left and right found new support. (See the following chapters for details on all these points.) Democratic capitalism, said many observers, was on its last legs.

The system was not on the way out, but it was changing. Since the beginning of the industrial revolution, governments realized that they had a duty to intervene to protect citizens from the harsher effects of the free market. For example, laws were passed to limit child labor and protect the quality of manufactured food. By the end of the 1930s, the scope of acceptable intervention had been widened.

Even moderate politicians talked not only of regulating the economy more tightly, but even of taking over its "commanding heights." In the 1920s such talk would have been considered dangerously anti-democratic. The way was open for key industries to be taken over by the government and for the state to undertake looking after its citizens "from the cradle to the grave."

A DIVIDED CULTURE

The 1920s are commonly described as "roaring." The popular image — largely drawn from the U.S. — is of new wealth, parties, jazz, daring clothes, and a sensational craving for enjoyment. Needless to say, this was only a tiny part of the story. For the bulk of people, trapped in dull, poorly-paid jobs, the twenties did not roar, they whimpered or moaned. But there was a feeling that, with a bit of luck, things could improve.

(As) the capitalist system crumbles . . . before our eyes . . . hundreds of poets, novelists . . . and . . . writers recognize the necessity of personally helping to accelerate the destruction of capitalism and the establishment of a workers' government . . . Communism must come and must be fought for.

Declaration of the American Writers' Congress, 1935.

The most magnificent picture ever!

DAVID O. SELZNICK'S PRODUCTION OF MARGARET MITCHELL'S

"GONE WITH THE WIND"

Winner of Ten Academy Awards

STARRING
**CLARK GABLE
VIVIEN LEIGH
LESLIE HOWARD OLIVIA de HAVILLAND**

A SELZNICK INTERNATIONAL PICTURE · DIRECTED BY VICTOR FLEMING · SCREEN PLAY BY SIDNEY HOWARD · METRO-GOLDWYN-MAYER INC. · RE-RELEASED BY MUSIC BY MAX STEINER

G GENERAL AUDIENCES

METROCOLOR ®   MGM 🦁 T United Artists

Throughout the Depression the movie industry continued to provide an hour or two of happiness for those who could afford the price of a ticket to the movies. Gone With the Wind *(1939) was perhaps Hollywood's greatest creation of the period.*

American novelist John Steinbeck (1902-1968) after receiving the Nobel Prize for Literature in 1962. His novels In Dubious Battle *(1936),* Of Mice and Men *(1937), and* The Grapes of Wrath *(1939) awoke the nation's conscience to the plight of migrant farmworkers in the 1930s.*

This optimism evaporated with the onset of the Great Depression. The impact on culture was twofold. On one hand it produced realistic art and literature that reflected the uncertainty of the times — fractured, tortured paintings, pessimistic philosophy, and sad novels of poverty and injustice. On the other hand, it increased the market for escapism, especially through film.

The movies sold sweet dreams. Anyone with a few cents could enter a warm, shimmering picture palace and be transported to a never-never world of beauty, romance, or unimaginable wealth. It was all a million miles from life as the viewer knew it. By the end of the decade color added its own magic. The same stories were told over and over again — rags to riches, boy meets girl, the good guy triumphs in the end. Many movies were poor. Some — *Gone With the Wind* (1939) being the most famous — were magnificent. All helped the audience to forget.

The intellectual response to the Depression and its consequences may be shown by three works: Picasso's *Guernica* was painted in 1937 after the bombing of a Spanish town of that name. The huge canvas is a powerful protest against the violence that arose out of the slump. Its cubist style suggests isolation, bewilderment, and fragmentation.

Frenchman Paul Valéry's *Glimpses of the Modern World* (1931) argued that Europeans were abandoning the three traditional pillars of Western civilization: Roman law, Greek humanity, and Christian sensitivity to the needs of others.

The Grapes of Wrath, written in 1939 by the American author John Steinbeck, is better known. It concentrated on the effect of massive recession in the lives of ordinary people. The novel was based on first-hand observation and had a huge impact when it was published. It is not overtly political. Instead, readers of the novel are left to draw their own conclusions about the effects of the Depression.

POLITICAL UPHEAVAL

Responses to the Great Depression varied greatly from country to country. A few were virtually untouched by the global catastrophe. Some recovered swiftly without undergoing political upheaval. Others recovered only after a total collapse of their political system. Most major states experienced a disturbing period of instability, followed by a gradual upturn. Two countries, Japan and Italy, responded to the Depression with aggressive expansion overseas.

THE VARIETY OF RESPONSES

The USSR was hardly affected by the Great Depression. The country was outside the international banking system, and its economy was largely self-sufficient. Nor did the slump have a profound impact on Third World countries (largely in Asia) whose economies depended little on international trade. The response in developing countries attached to a European empire depended largely on the policy of the "mother" country. The British, for example, demanded that their country's colonies should balance their budgets. This caused considerable hardship, particularly in India.

Reactions in industrialized states were equally diverse. Some, such as Sweden and Japan, adopted Keynesian policies (see page 44) early on and recovered rapidly. At the other extreme was France, which kept the franc on the gold standard until 1935 and underwent much hardship as a result. The United States, boosted by President Roosevelt's New Deal, began to recover in 1933. By 1936, believing the worst was over, Roosevelt began cutting government spending and relief programs that had been set up to counter the Depression. As a result, the country slipped into another recession in 1937-1938.

Britain's application of Keynes' policies was more cautious. Nevertheless, helped by spending on rearma-

We have indeed before us only the alternatives of collective leadership, collective control, or chaos . . . .

A. Salter, British economist, 1933.

In 1936 Spain slid into a civil war between the Republicans and the Nationalists. Many left-wing volunteers from other countries fought for the Republicans in the international brigades. This picture shows Republican and international brigade fighters in the front line.

ment, the country was almost out of recession by the outbreak of World War II. Overall, Europe recovered more quickly than the U.S. By 1937 it handled over 50 percent of world trade, compared with America's 16 percent.

The Depression had the most important political consequences in countries whose governments were least secure. Recession alone did not bring about political collapse. But the discontent it created gave anti-democrats the chance they needed. The most famous example of this was Hitler's rise to power in Germany. The slump also helped undermine democracy in Japan, Spain, and several smaller countries.

DEPRESSION AND INSTABILITY

With the fall of the dictator Primo de Rivera in 1930, Spain enjoyed a brief period of democratic rule until the outbreak of civil war in 1936. The causes of the conflict were many and complex. Moreover, the Depression had less effect in Spain than in many other European countries. It did play a part in destabilizing the country, however. Spain's traditional exports, notably citrus fruits and minerals,

declined sharply. Secondly, after 1932 many Spanish emigrants returned home looking for work. These changes increased working-class unemployment and poverty, producing a situation in which extremists flourished.

The postwar peace settlements established or reestablished a number of European countries with democratic systems of government. In the years that followed, democracy had a hard time of it. Poland and Lithuania became virtual dictatorships in 1926. The Great Depression hastened the fall of democracy in several other states. King Carol II imposed a right-wing regime on Romania in 1930. The recession also added to the problems of Yugoslavia, where King Alexander I was assassinated in 1934.

At the height of the Depression, neo-fascist regimes took control of the Baltic republics of Latvia and Estonia. In Italy, where the Fascist dictator Benito Mussolini had been in power since 1922, unemployment rose and exports fell. The situation was not helped by Mussolini's determination to maintain the value of the lira. It was finally devalued in 1936. Opposition in a totalitarian state was almost impossible, however, and in 1935 Mussiolini sought to divert attention away from his domestic troubles by invading Abyssinia (now called Ethiopia) in Africa.

The Depression also turned the Japanese toward overseas adventure. As a great trading nation, Japan was hit soon and hard by the recession. The situation was made worse by the government's ill-timed decision to return to the gold standard in June 1929. Exports fell from 2.5 billion yen in 1929 to 1.4 billion yen in 1931. Raw silk prices dropped by approximately 65 percent. Rice prices fell by only slightly less. Like other industrial nations, Japan was confronted with unemployment, bankruptcies, and poverty.

Political extremism fed on discontent. A right-wing youth shot the Japanese prime minister in 1930. The proudly nationalist military increased its influence in political affairs, leading to the invasion of the Chinese province of Manchuria in 1931. When the action was condemned by the League of Nations, Japan left the League. Within a few years Japan had sided with the European Fascist powers and made further inroads into China.

Ironically, Japan made perhaps the swiftest recovery from the Depression of any industrial nation. The yen was devalued, interest rates were reduced, and

We reject the capitalist system, which disregards the needs of the people . . . All Spanish citizens are entitled to employment.

From the party manifesto of Spain's right-wing Falange party, 1934.

government spending increased. It came too late to repair the damage done to its fragile democracy. As in Germany, right-wing militarism and extreme nationalism had taken a grip on the country that only defeat in war would break.

AUTARKY

A uniformed relief worker ladles out free soup to the German destitute in 1931. The following year millions of Germans expressed their disillusionment with the system that had brought them such misery by voting for Adolf Hitler.

The economic downturn began to affect Germany as early as 1928. Six months before the Wall Street Crash, the country already had 2 million unemployed. Between 1929 and 1933 exports fell by 54 percent and total industrial production by 34 percent. Unemployment, as we have seen, was higher than in either the U.S. or Britain.

Since 1919 Germany had been a democratic republic (the Weimar Republic). Because its democratic politicians were associated with the injustices of the Treaty of Versailles, reparations, and the soaring inflation of the mid-1920s, they were not widely respected. When they reacted to the Depression in traditional ways (cutting social services, benefits, and salaries),

their popularity fell further. In contrast, the appeal of extreme politicians – notably Hitler's Nazis — grew. They promised national unity, prosperity, and full employment. Hitler also claimed to know the cause of the Depression — cynical manipulation by greedy Jewish bankers.

Nazi strength at the polls rose in parallel with unemployment. When the number out of work was highest (July 1932), they won 230 seats out of 608 in the German Reichstag (parliament). The following January Hitler was invited to become chancellor of Germany. Within a year the democratic system that had brought him to power was in ruins.

Hitler restored the German economy. The policy he followed became known as "autarky." It involved government direction of the economy, rejecting open, worldwide trade, and making the country as self-sufficient as possible. Foreign goods were kept out by high tariffs. The government encouraged the use of substitutes in place of imported goods. Synthetic oil, for example, was produced from coal, and recycling was actively supported. Rearmament and the jobs that it created resulted in a reduction in the number of unemployed.

Autarky was the official policy in Japan, Fascist Germany, and Italy. However, it also influenced thinking in democratic countries. The French government, for example, managed agricultural production to reduce the output of luxuries and increase that of basic foodstuffs.

Helped by autarky and high government expenditure, particularly on armaments, German unemployment fell steadily. The specter of starvation dissolved. By 1939 virtually everyone who wished to work could do so. Manufacturing output and domestic consumption rose.

Experts are divided over the true strength of the German recovery. To some extent it was indeed artificial — expenditure on armaments could not go on rising forever, and the country experienced serious difficulties with its balance of payments. But to millions of average Germans that was relatively unimportant. What really mattered was that the Great Depression had been conquered, and its impact on their lives had ceased. National pride, which had been so badly damaged by Germany's defeat in World War I, was finally restored. Once again, Germany occupied a position of economic power in Europe.

The perils of Communism which seemed inexorably on the way, could be checked, Hitler persuaded us, and instead of hopeless unemployment, Germany could move toward economic recovery.

German architect and Nazi government official Albert Speer, 1931.

SURVIVAL

The countries where constitutional government was well established all survived the Great Depression with their political systems intact. But even the most stable societies, such as the U.S. and Britain, experienced considerable unrest. In France, where democracy had been on a roller coaster ride since the 1789 Revolution, the system was more seriously threatened. At times during the 1930s, the French Third Republic seemed close to collapse.

Although the older democracies weathered the storm, the Depression had a big impact on attitudes and policy. However, because of the outbreak of European war in 1939, the full effect of the new thinking did not become apparent until the 1950s. This chapter examines the shorter-term responses to the Depression in the more important democracies outside the U.S.

FRANCE

The figures show the approximate percentage of a country's work force registered unemployed. The actual percentages were higher still, particularly in Germany and France. The figures for France, where a high proportion of the work force were still engaged in agriculture, do not give a true indication of the hardship brought about by the Depression.

France's political system made it almost impossible for strong leadership to emerge. At the heart of the problem lay proportional representation, which awarded parties representation in parliament roughly in proportion to the number of votes they won. This led to a rapid growth of political parties. Governments were formed out of coalitions made up of several groups. The loss of loyalty of one small party, representing only a fraction of the population, could bring about a change of government. Between the two World Wars, France had 44 governments and 20 prime ministers.

Unemployment Figures				
	US	GERMANY	BRITAIN	FRANCE
1920	4%	10%	13%	3%
1928	4%	13%	12%	2%
1932	25%	44%	23%	3.5%
1935	20%	12%	17%	5%
1938	19%	2%	13%	4%

Instead of a few broad parties, as in Britain or the U.S., French political parties spread across the political spectrum, from far right to far left. Parties on the right formed the *bloc national*. Those of the left made up a *bloc des gauches* (later the *front populaire*). The balance of power was often held by the radical-socialists, whose policies tended to be unclear.

Understandably, given the instability of the system, the Great Depression caused chaos in France. Its full effects were not felt until 1932, when a left-wing coalition had just come to power. It lacked decisive leadership and was prevented by business interests from devaluing the franc. Between May 1932 and February 1934, six leftist governments watched as unemployment rose to 1.3 million and exports decreased. Traditional policies, such as cutting the salaries of civil servants, only made the recession worse.

Support for political extremism grew. The right compared France's sorry state with the revival taking place in Nazi Germany. In February 1936 various right-wing groups combined to attack the legislative assembly. They were beaten off by police, leaving 15 dead and over 300 injured. When Leon Blum came to power in 1936 at the head of a broad radical and left-wing coalition (the *front populaire*), it looked as if things might improve. The franc was devalued and wages raised. Sadly, any benefits these policies might have brought were undermined by inflation and a wave of strikes.

France's internal problems had serious international repercussions. First, they delayed rearmament in the face of the growing power of Germany. Secondly, no government was strong enough to take decisive action when, in 1936, Hitler began to break the Treaty of Versailles by sending troops into the Rhineland, then occupied by France. French weakness, stemming in part from the Great Depression, was an important factor in the international situation that led to war in 1939.

All humanism has an element of weakness, owing to its hatred of fanaticism, its tolerance, and its fondness for . . . skepticism — in other words, its natural goodness . . . What we need today is militant humanism.

German writer Thomas Mann, 1938.

BRITAIN

During the 1920s, the British economy was marked by high unemployment and sluggish growth. Politically the most interesting development was the replacement of the Liberal Party by the socialist Labour Party as the chief opposition to the right-wing Conservative Party. Labour formed its first government in 1924 and came to power again in 1929. It was hardly a favorable time for political experiment.

Labour Prime Minister Ramsay MacDonald, advised by civil service economists, rejected the Keynesian proposals put forward by extremist politicians. Instead, he tried to apply traditional remedies to the problem of recession. Unemployment rose alarmingly, reaching a desperate 80 percent in some towns. In 1931, a special committee advised cuts in government expenditure. Most Labour politicians, elected to support the lot of the workers, refused to accept the committee's recommendations. In August the prime minister and his cabinet resigned.

Instead of calling an election, MacDonald joined with Liberals and Conservatives to form a National Government. This government received overwhelming support in the general election of October 27, 1931. The National Government, soon dominated by Conservatives, attempted to tackle the slump with traditional policies. Expenditure was cut and benefits were subjected to a "means test." This meant that the amount of benefit given depended on the circumstances of each recipient.

The new thinking did have some effect. Britain came off the gold standard in 1931, and in 1934,

The Jarrow "Crusade," 1936. To draw attention to their destitute condition, a group of unemployed men from Jarrow in northeast England marched to London. Their discipline and good-heartedness made a lasting impression on the nation's conscience.

£2 million of relief was to be shared by the areas most depressed. Unemployment fell below two million in 1936, and in 1940 it was under a million for the first time since 1921. Even so, the upturn was spotty. In areas dominated by traditional industries a high proportion of the work force remained without jobs until World War II. When improvement eventually came, it was due more to increased production of armament and other supplies for the armed forces and to the worldwide recovery than to government policy.

As in France, the Depression in Britain had important political consequences. The discredited and divided Labour Party remained out of power until 1945. At the height of the crisis, extremist groups on both the left and right grew in popularity. The Communist Party attracted little support at elections, but exercised influence through the protests of the National Unemployed Workers' Movement. A British Union of Fascists was organized by a disillusioned extremist, Oswald Mosley, in 1932. Its violent demonstrations and anti-Semitic views attracted media attention but limited popular support.

In the longer term, the Great Depression played a part in Britain's failure to resist German expansion in the 1930s. Memories of the slump also exercised a powerful influence over postwar British policy. (This is discussed in the final chapter of the book).

THE SMALLER DEMOCRACIES

By and large the smaller democracies seemed better able to protect their people from the effects of the Depression than the larger ones. In some areas, Scandinavia for example, this was because socialist governments gave welfare top priority. In the first half of the century real wages rose more quickly in Sweden than in any other European country. Even so, the picture in northern Europe was not universally rosy. With the exception of the years 1930-1932, Norway's unemployment remained consistently higher than Germany's.

As in the larger states, extreme right-wing groups flourished briefly during the worst years of the Depression. They were perhaps strongest in Belgium, the Netherlands, and Finland. By 1939, they were all losing influence. The most lasting effect of the recession on the smaller democracies was the acceptance by

An army of unemployed led by millionaires quoting the Sermon on the Mount – that is our danger . . . The Lady in the Rolls Royce car is more damaging to morale than a fleet of Goering's bombing planes.

English novelist and essayist George Orwell, 1941.

We have no territorial demands to make in Europe.

Adolf Hitler, 1936

almost all political parties of the need for more sympathetic social legislation.

Czechoslovakia's economic difficulties had more tragic consequences. Carved out of the Austro-Hungarian Empire after World War I, the country was a rare example of a new democracy that worked. Tension remained, however, between the different peoples that made up the new republic. The largest groups were the Czechs and the Slovaks. There were also several million German-speakers, living mostly in the Sudetenland, an industrial province in the northwest adjacent to Germany.

The Depression heightened the wish of the Sudeten Germans to be reunited with Germany. They felt, perhaps incorrectly, that they were being economically held back by the need to support more rural areas farther to the east. They also compared their own slow recovery with Germany's rapid development. Dissatisfaction was further whipped up by Nazi propaganda. The tragic outcome was an enforced partition, or division, of Czechoslovakia and later surrender to German control in 1938-1939.

The Depression had a similar effect in Austria. Following the collapse of the country's main bank in 1931, the country was plunged into what was virtually a civil war between Socialists and Fascists. German troops entered Vienna on March 13, 1938. The *Anschluss*, or union with Germany, that was proclaimed received widespread popular support.

The democratic British ex-colonies of Canada, Australia, and New Zealand all suffered from the effects of the Depression. Canada was very badly hit by the worldwide slump in grain prices. In the early stages of the recession there was serious talk in Australia of cutting all links with Britain. The matter was never put to a referendum, however, and gradually faded. By the end of the decade Australian manufacturing industries were leading a modest economic recovery.

Saviors of the world? Fascism was often presented as a solution to the problems associated with the Depression. In this Nazi propaganda poster of 1933, Fascist leaders Adolf Hitler and Benito Mussolini are portrayed as guardian angels.

AMERICA RESPONDS TO DEPRESSION

Herbert Hoover was elected as U.S. president in November 1928. He was a humane man. The devastating effects of the Depression hurt him deeply; his concern for the starving was genuine. He was a diligent man, too. He often worked 18 hours a day, making himself overweight, red-eyed, and hoarse. But nothing he did or said made much difference.

Hoover lost the confidence of the people. How could they trust a man who said the "fundamental business" of America was "on a sound and prosperous basis" when shares in US Steel were falling from $262 to $22 each? When unemployment rose from 3.25 million in March 1930 to 13 million in 1932? When he ignored a petition signed by 1,000 economists and signed the Hawley-Smoot Tariff? When new automobile sales fell from 4.5 million (1929) to 1 million (1932)? When he praised individual states for their relief work but refused to allow the federal government to do anything similar?

The Republican President's optimistic statements, designed to restore confidence, rebounded cruelly. Hoover was held responsible for the Depression. Shanty towns of tin and cardboard became known as "Hoovervilles." Newspaper bedding for the homeless was the "Hoover blanket." In the fall elections of 1930 the Republicans did badly, losing control of the House of Representatives and hanging onto the Senate by only one seat.

Still the recession deepened. In 1931, 2,298 banks were ruined. Farmers left sheep dead in the fields because they did not have the money to transport them to market. Starving families picked their way through garbage heaps, looking for edible scraps. The homeless bedded down next to municipal incinerators for warmth. Charities and relief services simply could not cope with the enormity of the task before them.

We are nearer today to the ideal of the abolition of poverty and fear from the lives of men and women than ever before in any land.

Presidential campaign speech of Herbert Hoover, 1928.

The Government should assist and encourage . . . movements of collective self-help by itself cooperating with them.

U.S. President Hoover's reaction to the downturn in the U.S. economy.

I pledge you, I pledge myself, to a new deal for the American people.

F.D. Roosevelt, during presidential campaign, 1932.

Hoover's message — that the robust individualism of the American citizen would see the country through until the economy recovered — fell on deaf ears. The old ways were no longer good enough. New problems required new solutions or, in the words of Democratic presidential candidate Franklin Delano Roosevelt, a "New Deal." In November 1932, by 22,815,539 votes to 15,759,930, the American people accepted Roosevelt's offer.

Inauguration Day, March 4, 1933, was a bank holiday. But not an official one. Major banks refused to open for business for fear they would be ruined. Whatever the new President had to offer, he was not going to have an easy time of it.

THE NEW DEAL

F.D.R. greets a mine worker on the campaign trail, 1932. Governor Franklin D. Roosevelt ran for the presidency by offering a New Deal for Depression-hit America.

The most famous response to the Great Depression was President Franklin D. Roosevelt's package of measures known as the New Deal. One particularly devastating effect of the Depression in the U.S. was the undermining of the nation's morale. Since the Revolution, America had prided itself on being the

land of opportunity. Millions had flocked here in search of prosperity and freedom. And, for the most part, they had found it. Now the dream was shattered. The land of the fresh start was looking like a dead end.

Roosevelt's genius lay in understanding this mood. His New Deal was criticized by conservatives as being too radical. The left said it did not go far enough. Today scholars agree that it was far less radical than it appeared. To some extent, however, the substance of the package was less important than its message.

The President told Americans that they could conquer the Depression just as they had beaten the British and tamed the West. Even if his actions did little to restore prosperity, they restored hope. That, at the time, was perhaps more important than anything else. (It was not until World War II that the U.S. began to recover from the Depression.)

After he had been in office for some time, President Roosevelt said that the three aims of his New Deal had been Relief, Recovery, and Reform. This gave his policy a consistency it never had in practice. Roosevelt was nothing if not a politician. He knew that to stay in power and get anything done, he had to keep the support of the many and often conflicting sections of American society — business, agriculture, industrial labor, lawyers, small businesses, federal and state employees, and so forth. His New Deal, therefore, was a diverse series of measures — some quite radical, some conventional, very few actually new.

In order to bring immediate relief, Roosevelt's federal administration, supported by the Democratic Congress, launched a series of short-term measures. Banks were put on a sounder footing, farmers were helped to pay off their mortgages, and a Civilian Conservation Corps was set up to give work to young men. Considerable federal funds were also made available for public works and state projects.

In the spring of 1933 Congress passed a flood of new laws with unprecedented speed. Not all of them helped recovery. We now know that the way out of a recession is for government to borrow money and spend. This is the key to recovery. The Economy Act of 1933, however, implied that government over-spending had been a cause of the Depression. Roosevelt even declared that the age of U.S. economic expansion was over. On the other hand, a newly established Home Owners Loan Corporation (1933) gave out 300,000 new loans in a year to help people buy their own homes.

So first of all let me assert my firm belief that the only thing we have to fear is fear itself . . . .

From President Roosevelt's inaugural address, Washington, March 4, 1933.

The National Industrial Recovery Act (NIRA, 1933) sought to please both sides of industry. It recognized the rights of the work force by permitting workers to join unions, to bargain over wage increases and to go on strike. Industrial leaders were called upon to work together to establish standards for the quality of goods, prices and working hours. The Agricultural Adjustment Act of 1933 offered farmers subsidies in return for reducing the number of acres that they farmed. With great reluctance, the President also took the dollar off the gold standard. As a result, the value of the dollar fell, making U.S. exports a better buy overseas.

Reform meant trying to make the economic scene more just. To some extent this was accomplished by the banking reforms, closer control of the stock market, and the powers given to labor in the NIRA. The National Housing Act (1933) was passed to create both work and a better standard of housing.

Roosevelt's most radical move was probably the establishment of the Tennessee Valley Authority in 1933. The Authority remodeled an entire river valley, generating electricity, improving navigation, and controlling floods in one of the nation's poorest areas.

THE SECOND NEW DEAL

The rush of measures passed during the "first hundred days" of 1933 were followed by a second wave during 1934-1936. These included the establishment of a Securities and Exchange Commission (1934) to oversee the stock market, a Resettlement Administration (1935) to help tenant farmers obtain their own land and equipment, and a Works Progress Administration (1935) to provide employment in public works such as the construction of schools and roads. The National Labor Relations Board (1935) tried to curb unfair practices at work, while the Social Security Act (1935) set up a system of sickness and unemployment insurance and old age pensions. A Trade Agreements Act (1934) gave the President power to stimulate trade by negotiating lower tariffs.

Government has to be finally responsible for the well-being of its people. If private business fails . . . those suffering hardship . . . . have a right to call upon the government for aid.

U.S. President Roosevelt, explaining the need for his New Deal, Washington, 1932.

The list of government measures makes impressive reading. It represents a complete change in the way Americans thought about their government. As we will see, in the long run this change in Americans' thinking was probably of greater consequence than the economic recovery it announced.

REACTIONS TO THE NEW DEAL

From Roosevelt's point of view, the New Deal was an outstanding success. As the first President to seek more than two terms in office, he was actually reelected three times. The economic consequences of his measures, however, were less impressive. The U.S. did not lift itself out of recession until the economy was stimulated by the outbreak of World War II in 1939. The political consequences of the Roosevelt administration were much more dramatic. It altered forever the balance of power between the federal and state governments and left the President with greatly enhanced authority.

THE ECONOMIC EFFECTS OF THE NEW DEAL

In economic terms the New Deal had only a limited impact. Unemployment fell by more than a million between 1933 and 1934, but it still remained unacceptably high. Although $3 billion was eventually

The blue eagle was the symbol of the National Recovery Administration. This was the first of the New Deal programs. It was intended to limit the production of goods and discourage competition between businesses.

I fear it may end the progress of a great country and bring its people to the level of the average European.

Republican senator Daniel Hastings criticizes the New Deal.

distributed in emergency relief, this did little to tackle the underlying problems of the U.S. Agriculture was hit by a terrible drought in 1934. A second wave of recession, known as the "Roosevelt Depression," rocked the country between 1937 and 1938. By 1939 there were still ten million workers without jobs. Older industries, such as the textile industry, remained depressed. At the end of the decade the U.S. share of world trade remained lower than it had been in the 1920s.

Nevertheless, the slide into chaos had been halted and there was limited recovery. Newer industries, such as the manufacture of consumer goods, picked up well. The Works Progress Administration created 8.5 million jobs, although many of these were short-term. As a result, there were over 664,000 miles (1 million km) of new roads built, 122,000 new public buildings and 285 new airports. The currency settled to 60 percent of its former value, allowing overseas trade to recover. The capitalist system had survived, even though in a rather different form. After ten years of painful readjustment, the U.S. was in position to resume its role as the engine of world prosperity.

The political repercussions of the New Deal were many and varied. It led to a constitutional battle between the President and the Supreme Court. In 1935 the conservative court declared measures such as the NIRA to be unconstitutional. The President responded by asking Congress for the power to appoint new judges. The crisis was ended when some of the more traditionally-minded judges retired and previous anti-New Deal decisions were reversed.

As in Europe, the government's inability to reverse the Depression swiftly increased communism's popularity. Although the Communist Party polled only slightly over 100 thousand votes in the 1932 presidential election (its greatest success), radical left-wing thinking influenced a number of U.S. intellectuals. More significant was the rise of organized labor, helped by the NIRA. Between 1933 and 1939, trade union membership rose threefold. In 1937, there was a series of crippling strikes, some marked by unpleasant violence.

Roosevelt didn't follow any particular policy after 1936 . . . . It was the War that saved the economy and saved Roosevelt.

Columbia professor of law, Raymond Morley, sacked from the Roosevelt administration in 1936, later criticized the president for not doing more to regulate business.

The New Deal brought the Democratic Party out of the political wilderness. A new coalition of northern liberals and southern conservatives kept the party in power until 1953. Long before this, however, the New Deal had been abandoned. By 1937, alarmed by labor unrest and the mounting deficit ($4 billion), Roosevelt was swinging back to more conservative policies. He cut government spending and backed few radical measures. The Fair Standards Labor Act of 1938, which limited child labor and set up a minimum wage, is generally reckoned to be the last gasp of the New Deal.

THE RISE OF THE MODERN PRESIDENCY

The New Deal began the era of what has been called the "imperial Presidency." The measures of 1933-1938 alone were not responsible for the increase in presidential authority. Among other factors, the powers acquired by the national leader during World War II were also important. Nevertheless, Roosevelt set the process in motion.

Roosevelt made himself the focus of the nation's attention. He spoke to the electorate directly through his famous "fireside chats" on the radio. As the federal government grew — the number of federal employees almost doubled between 1933 and 1939 — so did the authority of its head. The President was empowered to negotiate trade deals. He was given vast sums to spend as he thought fit. The Public Works Administration, for example, was granted $3.3 billion for public works projects.

Finally, the Great Depression and the New Deal brought home the message that the U.S. had a national economy that needed national direction. As a last resort, the only person capable of giving that direction was the President.

Depression leads to violence. Striking Ohio dairy workers overturn a milk truck that is trying to break their strike, 1935. By the mid-1930s the U.S. government was alarmed by mounting industrial unrest and adopted a less conciliatory attitude toward workers' demands.

LONG-TERM CONSEQUENCES

The Great Depression marked a turning point in the history of the twentieth century. The instability it generated was an important long-term cause of World War II. It set out the ground rules for economic and social policy in all major non-Communist countries for almost 50 years. Its effects on many aspects of society, from the right to work to the moral responsibilities of wealth, continue to influence human behavior to the present day.

WORLD WAR II

World War II grew out of the Great Depression. A number of forces were at work. Recession bred dissatisfaction with governments in power. Where these were democracies, desperate people turned to extremist groups that promised prosperity and restored national pride. Food and work, for the moment, were more important than votes or rights. Thus the military eased themselves into positions of power in Japan and the Nazis took over Germany.

The right-wing regimes' need for armaments boosted their economies and so helped economic recovery. They also had no scruples about using military force to extend the markets for domestic goods or seize supplies of raw materials. The Japanese first occupied Manchuria and then went on to conquer much of eastern China. Mussolini sent Italian troops to occupy Abyssinia (Ethiopia). Hitler took over Austria, Czechoslovakia, and, in 1939, Poland.

Democratic states, most of which were still opposed to massive increases in spending, were slow to rearm. President Roosevelt did not agree to large-scale U.S. spending on armaments until 1939. This attitude rendered the democracies incapable of resisting right-wing aggression. The method advocated by the League of Nations — economic sanctions — was doomed to failure at a time when merchants were desperate to increase

The Pacific peril. The front cover of Ken *magazine, May 1938, warning that Japan was threatening U.S. interests by secretly advancing into the Pacific.*

sales. Not only did the Depression bring aggressive regimes to power, therefore, but it deprived their opponents of the means with which to resist them.

INTERNATIONAL COOPERATION

The world economy recovered from the Great Depression. In the process much was learned about how to prevent a similar recession from returning. Remembering how an impoverished Germany had embraced political extremism in the 1930s, after World War II, the U.S. pumped $12.5 billion into Western Europe. This built up the war-torn democracies and enabled them to resist the advance of Communism.

Memories of the Depression also played a part in the formation of the European Union. This began as an organization for economic cooperation (the European Steel and Coal Community), grew into the

European Economic Community, and is now a socio-economic bloc of huge wealth and international influence. Some "Euro-skeptic" politicians, such as Britain's Margaret Thatcher, complain that the EU threatens national sovereignty. The EU defense is that a little loss of national identity is better than a return to the international misery of the Great Depression and World War II.

The General Agreement on Tariffs and Trade (GATT), a specialist agency of the United Nations, was established in 1948 to promote international trade. It became permanent in 1960 and by 1990 had 96 member states. Remembering the lessons of the Depression, it has been quite successful in negotiating agreements to keep down protective tariffs in order to keep world trade flowing.

The International Monetary Fund (IMF), another UN agency, was set up in 1946. Member states subscribe to it according to their wealth. The funds are used to help states out of short-term difficulties. The World Bank is a third UN agency established after World War II to make a major recession less likely. For the first years of its existence it gave huge loans at low rates of interest. These tended to build up debts that could never be repaid, discouraging further investment. Recently it has followed more monetarist policies (see page 69). Following the Brandt Report of 1977, highlighting the widening gap between the developed economies and the rest of the world, the Bank has helped with debt repayment and concentrated funds on smaller, technological projects.

We the people of the United Nations [are] determined . . . to employ international machinery for the promotion of the economic and social advancement of all peoples.

From the Charter of the United Nations.

SOCIAL DEMOCRACY

World War II increased the power of central governments in all combatant countries. This accentuated a trend begun during the Depression. Although there was deregulation after the war, particularly in the U.S., there was no return to the *laissez-faire* economics of the 1920s. Most parties, particularly in Europe, accepted the need for social democracy. This meant running the country for the benefit of the mass of the electorate — curbing the excesses of competition and keeping taxes relatively high.

Many governments put key industries, such as the railroads, under state control. This enabled them to continue to operate when they were no longer economically viable. Jobs were preserved at the cost of losing out to more competitive economies.

By the 1950s, Keynesian economic policies were widely followed throughout the free world. Individual nations were worried less about debt than unemployment. Until the 1970s this resulted in handsome growth. It was found, however, that "pure" Keynesian policies — high government spending and low unemployment — brought problems of their own. They tended to boost the power of labor organizations. This enabled unions to demand wage increases that employers could not afford without raising prices. The result was inflation.

By the late 1970s a new economic orthodoxy emerged — monetarism. This rejected Keynesian theories and said that the key to economic management lay in controlling the amount of money in circulation. Two of the most notable monetarist governments were those of President Ronald Reagan in the U.S. and Prime Minister Margaret Thatcher in Britain. They both cut government spending, lowered taxes, and returned industries to private ownership. Competition, not cooperation was now all the rage. Inevitably, unemployment rose sharply.

Critics warned of a return to the days of the prewar slump. Monetarists pointed out that the problem of combined unemployment and inflation was something new and so needed new remedies. One thing was certain: whichever side one stood on, the reference point was the same — a determination never to repeat a tragedy on the scale of the Great Depression.

Old home, new hope. An African-American family gather before their home in Mississippi before being rehoused with the help of the federal government, 1938. The New Deal showed for the first time what a determined federal government could do to help the disadvantaged.

69

CONCLUSION

The Great Depression wrought economic havoc across the world. By 1931 it looked as if the whole capitalist system was on the verge of collapse. For a time there seemed no way of breaking the cycle of recession. Banks that had lost funds in the crash were unable to lend money to businesses. To save money employers laid off workers. The unemployed had to live off meager handouts. Thus fewer goods were bought, forcing employers to lay off more workers.

The social impact of the Depression was devastating. Throughout the world millions were thrown into poverty. Begging, illness, and crime increased. In some towns over half the work force was unemployed. Those with jobs accepted longer hours and lower wages. On occasion, workers' despair flared into violence. More often it resulted in depression and hopelessness.

Franklin D. Roosevelt (1882-1945), regarded by many as the greatest president the U.S. has ever had. During his presidency the federal government took on powers it has never since relinquished.

Less stable governments collapsed under the strain. The most famous example was Germany's Weimar Republic, which had governed the country since the end of World War I. Hitler's Nazis, offering work and glory, manipulated their way to power. They then set up a Fascist state that plunged Europe into war in 1939. Anxious to seize new markets and divert attention away from troubles at home, the right-wing governments of Japan and Italy also adopted aggressive foreign policies. The League of Nations, formed in 1919 to help international cooperation, was powerless to stop them.

Over time the Depression changed many governments' economic management. Accepting the theories of Maynard Keynes, they saw that economic affairs could not be left entirely in the hands of private business. The government had a responsibility to direct and regulate. The cycle of recession could be broken, for example, if governments borrowed to spend their way out of trouble. The Nazis achieved this with rapid rearmament. To a lesser extent, this was also the idea behind Roosevelt's reforms in the New Deal.

Keynesian economics increased the power of central government. President Roosevelt had far more influence over the lives of ordinary Americans than any previous peace-time president. Many European countries went further by putting major industries under state control. After World War II the U.S. pumped money into war-torn Europe to rebuild its economy and safeguard democracy.

The United Nations, which replaced the League of Nations, set up institutions (such as the World Bank and the International Monetary Fund) to help economic development and planning. The lasting lesson of the Great Depression was that prosperity and stability depended on international cooperation as much as competition.

YEARS OF DUST

RESETTLEMENT ADMINISTRATION
Rescues Victims
Restores Land to Proper Use

A Federal Resettlement Administration poster suggesting that Washington could help the victims of the "Dust Bowl." This parched region, including parts of Texas, Colorado, Oklahoma, New Mexico, and Kansas, was created by over-farming. During the crisis of 1933-1935 over 14.5 million acres (36 million ha) of farmland were devastated as 850 million tons of topsoil blew away, ruining thousands of farmers.

GLOSSARY

anti-Semitism
Prejudice or hostility toward Jews.

appeasement
The policy of keeping the enemy at bay by agreeing to some of their demands.

balance of payments
The difference between a nation's total income from and its total payments to foreign countries.

bankrupt
Unable to pay debts.

boom
Period of rapid economic development.

budget
Statement of income and expenditure.

capitalism
Economic system in which the means of production, distribution, and exchange are privately owned, and government direction is minimal.

civil service
Administrative services of a government.

civil war
War fought between groups of people or regions of the same country.

coalition
Government made up of more than one political party. Often a short-term alliance to achieve a special goal.

colony
Overseas territory conquered and governed by another country.

communism
Political system in which all property is collectively owned and the government takes control of nearly every aspect of life.

conference
A large meeting organized for the discussion of a specific subject.

credit
Financial borrowing.

currency
Money in use in a country.

deficit
Excess spending over income.

deflation
Increasing the value of money, which lowers prices.

democracy
Government by the people or their elected representatives.

devaluation
Lowering the value of currency in one country relative to that of other countries.

diplomacy
Management of relations between nations.

duty
Tax on goods being sold or transported.

economy
A country's finances, services, and industry.

electorate
Those with the right to vote.

empire
A widespread group of territories under the same government.

exports
Goods sold abroad by a country.

fascism
A political system that stresses nationalism and often a particular race over the individual and other races; usually led by a dictator.

foreign policy
A government's policy toward other nations.

free trade
Trading without import or export duties.

gold standard
A currency system by which the value of money was defined in terms of a fixed quantity of gold. The exchange rate between countries was determined by the value of their currency in gold.

Gross National Product (GNP)
The total value of a country's industry, trading, and commerce.

hyperinflation
Very high rate of inflation.

imperial
Relating to an empire.

imports
Goods a country buys from abroad.

inflation
Increase in prices and fall in the purchasing power of money.

investment
The investing of money in business or industry, usually by buying shares.

isolationism
A political system advocating the avoidance of all foreign alliances or other involvement in world affairs.

Keynesian
Following the theories of J. M. Keynes, who said that unemployment could be lowered by increased government spending.

laissez-faire
A doctrine or policy that opposes government interference or control of the economy.

League of Nations
Organization for international cooperation established at the Paris Peace Conference in 1919.

left wing
Tending toward socialism or liberalism.

liberalism
The political belief that emphasizes the individual and his or her civil and political rights.

monetarism
The belief that good economic management means controlling the amount of money in circulation.

oligopoly
The banding together of a few large companies to affect the market and prices.

protectionism
Introducing tariffs to protect domestic commerce from foreign competition.

rearmament
Building up military forces and supplies in preparation for war.

recession
An economic downturn.

referendum
The process by which the people of a country or state can vote directly on an issue, rather than following the usual course of voting through their elected representative.

reparations
Compensation paid by a country defeated in war to the victors.

revolution
Complete and rapid change, often taking the form of forcible action and resulting in a new ruler or system of government replacing the old power system.

right wing
Inclined toward capitalism and, in its extreme form, fascism.

services
Industries, such as catering and the media, that create jobs and wealth without manufacturing goods.

share
Financial investment resulting in a share of a business' profits. Owning a share is like owning a portion of the company.

slump
Deep recession.

socialism
A political system in which all means of production, distribution, and exchange are owned by the community rather than by individuals.

Soviet
Used to describe anything relating to the former Soviet Union.

Soviet Union
Union of Soviet Socialist Republics, the name given to Russia after Communist takeover in 1917.

speculation
To buy or sell stocks in the hope of making money through an expected rise or fall in their price.

stock
The money a company raises in return for a share in profits and other advantages of ownership.

stock exchange
A place where stocks and shares can be traded.

subsidize
To support or aid with public money.

subsidy
Money contributed by the state to bolster an organization or industry.

tariff
The tax on goods leaving or, in some cases, entering a country.

totalitarian
Under direct and complete control of an unelected government.

Wall Street
The New York Stock Exchange.

TIMELINE

1914 — World War I breaks out.

1917 — U.S. enters the war.
— The Communists seize power in Russia.

1918 — World War I ends.

1919 — The Treaty of Versailles is signed.
— The Weimar Republic takes power in Germany.
— Post-war recession in U.S. (to 1921).
— The League of Nations is founded.

1921 — German reparation payments are fixed at 132 billion gold marks.
— Warren G. Harding (Republican) becomes President.

1922 — The World Economic Conference is held in Geneva.
— The Fordney-McCumber Tariff is levied on goods imported to the U.S.
— Mussolini becomes prime minister of Italy.
— Allied debts to the U.S. total $11.5 billion.

1923 — French and Belgian troops occupy the Ruhr.
— Hyperinflation in Germany.

1924 — Calvin Coolidge (Republican) is elected as President of U.S.
— The Dawes Plan is launched, to ease German reparation payments.

1925 — Britain returns to the gold standard.

1926 — The General Strike in Britain.

1928 — Share prices are booming on Wall Street.
— U.S. overseas investment is falling.

1929 — Herbert C. Hoover (Republican) becomes President of U.S.
— Black Thursday and the Wall Street Crash – the beginning of the Great Depression.

1930 — The Hawley-Smoot Tariff is levied on imports to the U.S.
— The Young Plan further eases Germany's reparation payments.

— There is a global rise in unemployment.
— Raw material prices, trade, and industrial output are all falling worldwide.
— A right-wing regime takes power in Romania.

1931 — The Austrian State Bank fails.
— Britain leaves the gold standard and imposes import tariffs.
— Japan invades Manchuria.
— Britain's Labour prime minister forms a National Government.

1932 — The British Empire Conference agrees on "Imperial Preference."
— The Reconstruction Finance Corporation is set up in the U.S.
— 33 percent of all German workers are unemployed.
— 25 percent of all U.S. workers are unemployed.
— The British Union of Fascists is formed.

1933 — President Franklin D. Roosevelt of U.S. announces the New Deal, a package of measures formulated to alleviate the Depression in the U.S.
— U.S. leaves the gold standard.
— National Industrial Recovery Act (NIRA) in the U.S.
— The yen is devalued.
— The World Economic Conference is held in Geneva.
— Hitler becomes Chancellor of Germany.

1934 — Germany imposes import controls on all industrial goods.

1935 — Mussolini invades Abyssinia.
— The French mining industry is nationalized.
— The Social Security Act is passed in the U.S.

1936 — The devaluation of French franc, Swiss franc, and Italian lira.
— J. M. Keynes publishes *The General Theory of Employment, Interest, and Money*.
— Right-wing groups attack the French legislative assembly.
— The Spanish Civil War begins (to 1939).
— German troops occupy Rhineland.

1937 — Britain begins to rearm.
— A new recession in U.S. (to 1938).
— War breaks out between Japan and China.

1938 — Union between Germany and Austria.
— Germany takes Sudetenland from Czechoslovakia.

1939 — The U.S. increases expenditure on armaments.
— Germany invades Poland – beginning of World War II (to 1945).

1945 — The United Nations is established.

1946 — The International Monetary Fund (IMF) is set up.

1948 — The General Agreement on Trade and Tariffs (GATT) is set up.

1952 — The European Coal and Steel Community is set up.

1967 — The European Community (now European Union) is established.

FURTHER READING

Alexander, James E. *Depression Kids: Shaping the Character of Our Lives.* Macedon, 1993

Davies, Nancy M. *The Stock Market Crash of Nineteen Twenty-Nine* "American Events" series. Silver Burdett Press, 1994

Farell, Jacqueline. *The Great Depression.* Lucent Books, 1996

Fitzgerald, F. Scott. *The Great Gatsby.* Warner Books, 1995

Hacker, Jeffrey. *Franklin D. Roosevelt,* Marshall Cavendish, 1991

Hills, Ken. *1930s,* "Take Ten Years" series. Raintree Steck-Vaughn, 1993

Larsen, Rebecca. *Franklin D. Roosevelt: Man of Destiny,* Watts, 1991

Meltzer, Milton. *Brother, Can You Spare a Dime: The Great Depression 1929–1933.* Facts on File, 1990

Polikof, Barbara G. *Herbert C. Hoover: Thirty-First President of the United States,* Garrett Educational Corp., 1990

Ross, Stewart. *Causes and Consequences of World War II.* Raintree Steck-Vaughn, 1993

Sharman, Margaret. *1920s,* "Take Ten Years" series. Raintree Steck-Vaughn, 1993

Steinbeck, John. *The Grapes of Wrath.* Viking, Penguin, 1992

Stevens, Rita. *Calvin Coolidge: Thirtieth President of the United States,* Garrett Educational Corp., 1990

Stewart, Gail B. *The New Deal.* Silver Burdett Press, 1993

Terkel, Studs. *Hard Times: An Oral History of the Great Depression.* Pantheon Books, 1970

Wormser, Richard L. *Growing Up in the Great Depression.* Atheneum, Simon and Schuster Children's, 1994

INDEX

ACKNOWLEDGMENTS

The publishers are grateful to the following for permission to reproduce photographs:

Cover photo (large): The Granger Collection
Cover photo (small): Underwood & Underwood/ Corbis-Bettmann
The Mary Evans Picture Library, pages 6, 10, 14, 18, 22, 23, 25, 34, 35, 38, 42, 58; Corbis-Bettmann, pages 8, 12, 20, 28, 29, 45, 48, 52, 60, 65, 69; The Hulton Getty Picture Collection, pages 13, 17, 21, 24, 41, 50, 56; Peter Newark's American Pictures, pages 15, 16, 21, 27, 30, 33, 36, 37, 46, 47, 63, 67, 70, 71.